# Prosperity and Policy

## *Ireland in the 1990s*

Edited by

David Kennedy
and
Aidan Pender



Institute of Public Administration

First published 1990 by the Institute of Public Administration
57-61 Lansdowne Road, Dublin 4



ISBN 1 872002 00 5 paperback

Typeset by Corporate Graphics Limited, Dublin
Printed in the Republic of Ireland by the Leinster Leader Ltd.

# Contents

# Contributors

*Dr Marc Battaille* is president of the Swiss-based International Public Affairs Centre and chairman of a private agri-business group.

*Dr Hartmut Fest* is deputy director of the Economics and Statistics Department of the OECD, Paris.

*Dr Walter Grünsteidl* is advisor on international relations to the president of NV Philips Industries (The Netherlands). He previously was director of corporate strategic planning at Philips International.

*Mr Alan McCarthy* is chief executive of Coras Trachtala, the Irish Export Board.

*Mr Colm McCarthy* is a partner in the economic consultancy firm Davey, Kelleher, McCarthy and has recently worked with the Department of Finance on the review of public expenditure.

*Dr Aidan O'Boyle* is director of industrial policy in the Confederation of Irish Industry.

*Mr Albert Reynolds, TD,* is Minister for Finance.

*Dr Michael Walsh* is head of corporate finance and a director of the NCB Group.

AIDAN PENDER

# Introduction

THE papers published in this book represent the proceedings of a conference organised by the Institute of Public Administration in Dublin on 8 November 1989. The conference was the fifth annual public finance conference conducted by the Institute, a series that has established itself as a significant occasion on Ireland's business calendar. The conference sessions were chaired by Professor David Kennedy, deputy governor of the Bank of Ireland and ex-chief executive of Aer Lingus. Although the conference papers have been the subject of some revision and editing, the reader should note that they represent an analysis of the subject up to November 1989 and, particularly as they relate to certain economic variables, may have been overtaken by events since then.

As with most conferences, the organisers sought to reflect the essential subject matter of the proceedings within the terms of the conference theme. As we approached the conclusion of the 1980s, it seemed reasonable to turn our thoughts to the next decade, and to speculate on the type of Irish society which might emerge after a further ten years of economic and social evolution. It was also intended that the conference papers should provoke debate on the ways in which Irish society in the 1990s might seek to achieve vigorous economic growth, and a wider distribution of prosperity. In many respects, the economic debate of the 1980s was focused on our apparent inability as a nation to make substantial progress towards these ends. Despite the fact that there was much discussion about the policy directions that the Irish government might follow, there remained considerable uncertainty about the growth prospects of the economy and, in particular, its capacity to sustain the wide array of social needs that were articulated throughout the decade with increasing vigour and frequency. The issue, therefore, seemed to be one of achieving a measured degree of prosperity through the application of an equally measured set of policy initiatives. The opening of a new decade seemed to present a useful starting point for taking a fresh look at the more important and enduring of these economic and social issues.

Apart from enquiring into the relationship which could, or should, exist between prosperity and policy during the 1990s, the conference also sought to reflect a secondary theme which it was felt could, in time, come to characterise our development over the period. This was the theme of Ireland's even closer integration with the European Community (EC), and the consequences this might bring for the exercise of independently determined policy objectives. The implication, therefore, was that Ireland in the 1990s would emerge as a country which looked increasingly to the communities of mainland Europe for its reference points in relation to its social and economic development. This is not to suggest any potential diminution of those qualities which combine to characterise Ireland as a nation. It does suggest, however, that the process of economic policy harmonisation, which is now well under way within the EC, must inevitably involve the Irish people in formulating a new concept of what it means to be European, without necessarily requiring them to abandon existing concepts of what it means to be Irish.

Not surprisingly, therefore, this concept of a European interdependence emerged as a significant undercurrent to the conference proceedings, and was an issue which was explored in detail by a number of speakers. It is perhaps a measure of the speed with which events have been moving since the conference that, although there are some references to the changing political scene in Eastern Europe, the reader of these papers might feel that the impact of these events on Europe as a whole was not given sufficient consideration. It is worth recalling that in November 1989, such momentous events as the Romanian revolution, the talks on German unification, and the declaration of secession from the Soviet Union by Lithuania had not yet taken place. To the extent that such events could be said to have any influence upon developments in Ireland, their impact is most likely to be to remind us of the need for a strong European orientation in our future policy development.

As to be expected, many of the comments offered by the conference speakers centred around these themes of prosperity, policy and the European context within which these issues must necessarily be resolved. Dr Walter Gründsteidl (NV Philips

Industries), for example, offered a succinct overview of international trade development and, in particular, highlighted the immediate need for a combined European approach as a pragmatic response to the emergence of powerful global trading blocs. Both Mr Alan McCarthy (Córas Tráchtála) and Dr Michael Walsh (NCB Group) offered an Irish perspective on this issue and outlined the types of policy measures required to promote the further development of Irish industry, specifically the marketing strategies necessary for the expansion of Irish exports. The importance of people as a national resource emerges as a strong theme throughout the conference. Considerable emphasis was placed on this, both by Dr Marc Battaille (International Public Affairs Centre), who stressed the role of education as a primary characteristic in his portrait of the 'winning nation' and by Dr Aidan O'Boyle (Confederation of Irish Industry), who reasserted the need for continuing investment in education and technical skills, even if the application for such skills might not be found, in the first instance, within Ireland. Other aspects of labour market policy were dealt with by Dr Hartmut Fest (Organisation for Economic Co-operation and Development) who provided a comprehensive analysis of the potential within the Irish economy for employment creation, while Mr Colm McCarthy (DKM Group) offered some views on recent Irish macroeconomic performance and the future policy directions which he felt should be mapped out for the economy as we approached the 1990s.

The presentations, under the stewardship of Professor David Kennedy, contributed to a conference of thought-provoking analysis and stimulating discussion. It is hoped that those who take an interest in these matters will find the publication of the conference proceedings equally thought-provoking, and that some of the ideas to emerge from the book will serve as a sufficient reward for the time spent in reading it.

Institute of Public Administration
July 1990

ALBERT REYNOLDS

# Opening Address

IN its very title, this conference, 'Prosperity and Policy — Ireland in the 1990s', is provocative, but timely. You will forgive me if, in consequence, I follow a similarly provocative route in my remarks. Failure on my part to 'think afresh', I believe, would set this conference off on the wrong foot. Given the audience here today I know that those of you who operate outside the public sector will understand if I treat issues primarily with that arena in mind. But much of what I will say has wider application, of course.

Let me begin by suggesting that there is, sometimes, too little appreciation of the connection between prospects for 'prosperity' and the discharge of the 'policy' function. That the two are inextricably intertwined, you all well know.

The challenge for us is to evolve, and apply policy so as to underpin rather than undermine growth prospects. That in my view is the real measure of our commitment to Ireland and to our people's future. This applies both for the political decision-makers and for the public service managers and planners who assist in the policy process. Neither one nor the other can 'opt out' of responsibility to guide the country, in security, towards economic and social progress over the years ahead.

My responsibility, in the final analysis, is to decide upon budgetary and economic policy for the long-term good of all, not just for today's lobby. Whether your expertise is applied in a 'spending' or an 'economic' Department, or in a 'commercial' or 'public service' State enterprise, your advocacy will reflect a natural concern for your own particular clientele. But — and let us be quite clear about this — your responsibility requires that recommendations also embody a real regard for the well-being of the nation at large.

To properly discharge our respective responsibilities, then demands:

— that we see beyond the narrow impact of decisions on

our own particular clientele to their implications for the whole country;

— that we look beyond the short-term — addressing ourselves as much to tomorrow's needs as to today's;

— that we attune our thinking as much to impacts on economic fundamentals as to social, cultural or other effects of actions;

— that in coming to conclusions, we carefully weigh the balances, finding in favour of today only to the extent that doing so enhances Ireland's capacity for tomorrow.

What does all this mean, in practice? For the politician, it means having the courage to take the right course even if it is not the easier one. It means being ready to put up with unpopularity when the basis for medium-term social and economic advance demands the 'tough' decision. It means having a strategy for viable progress, and implementing that strategy — because it is best for the longer run — regardless of any political costs in the shorter term.

For the policy-advising public servant it means above all, exercising a broad judgement, taking account of the betterment of the whole community. To do this you have to be fully acquainted with the particular policy concerns and issues of your own field of responsibility. But you must also take account of the implications of your department's or corporation's actions on a much wider plane. It is quite insufficient now — indeed always was — that decisions be demonstrably in the immediate interests of any organisations's own 'customers'.

Whether we are politicians or advisers, we are not entitled to promote taxation, social, cultural, or other policies unless we are reasonably convinced that they are economically possible. To meet this test, policies — using my words of a few moments ago — must be judged in terms of their capacity to underpin rather than undermine the economic growth process. These judgements must be made in the light of reasonable rather than optimistic expectations about the economic and budgetary outlook, and they must be sustainable over time.

Ireland has had far to much of the 'one step forward' subsequently necessitating 'two steps back'. If a supposedly commercial proposition will not pay for itself, it is not commercial! If a social aspiration is not of a priority nature and if it needs budgetary funds which are not there — then we cannot afford it until we are producing the wealth to pay for it. If we disregard this fact of life we simply store up bills for the future.

Your approach must, therefore, place the present and future fundamental needs of the whole community ahead of the normally narrower goals of individual departments and corporations. You must explore and understand the total joint role of departments, and of ministers. You must look beyond the departmental position to the broader responsibility of the cabinet. You must aim to serve all the nation — rather than assume some perceived and unspoken, and probably inward-looking, stance on objectives.

Together, this is certainly how we have acted throughout the last couple of years. While we can take satisfaction from the results, in terms of a better performance, we should not carry this to the point of self-congratulation. If the 1990s are to be a decade of prosperity, the psychology of government and administration will have to undergo further change.

The stark reality is that, in the not too distant past, political and public service policy-makers either failed to look forward adequately to the consequences of recommendations and actions, or — more worryingly — failed to appreciate what those consequences might be. If in those years there was sufficient foresight and a proper appreciation of consequences, then there was a failure to bring public opinion to the same realisation. Looking back, you could say that in the past three years we have adopted policies which, while getting to grips with our present problems, are also geared towards safeguarding the future of our country.

As a nation, we ultimately had to face up to, and deal with, the reality of a rapidly rising, and intolerably large, National Debt. It has been the underlying factor in the retrenchment of public spending in recent years, and in our inability to make greater inroads into the burden of taxation. Equally, the private sector had to face up to the consequences of past pay awards which led to increases in product prices much higher than in competitor countries. Inevitably, job-security went out the window, and a vicious trend in redundancies set in. We reaped the whirlwind.

The task now is to ensure sustainable progress. For this we

must not only resolve never to repeat the mistakes of the past, but also to learn from them. This must be a common goal; it is not for me, nor for the cabinet, alone. Indeed, it is not for government and administration only, but for all in positions of leadership and decision-taking, in public and private sectors alike.

I have spoken about the need for a broadness of view. In this context I recall a quotation — perhaps not generally known, but one of which Ministers for Finance would be particularly aware. In the time of Louis XIV, the 'Sun King', Colbert defined as the best Minister for Finance, 'he who could pluck the goose of the greatest weight of feathers with the least amount of hissing'. When tax-bills arrive on your door-step, you may feel I subscribe to this view — but you would be wrong. This has never been my approach. In our circumstances today it would be a wholly inappropriate approach. The resulting condition of the goose must come into the reckoning. There is no point in plucking any bird, goose or hen to the point where she cannot lay tomorrow's breakfast egg!

What is tomorrow's breakfast? Above all, I see it as the capacity to offer productive employment to more and more of our people. We want to see more of our young people in a position to decide freely on a rewarding career here at home or, should they prefer — without being driven by unemployment — on an equally rewarding stint abroad. I want to see an economy that has the capacity, if we get things right, to tempt expatriates to return with new ideas and skills. There is another, similarly important, goal. It is the ability to pursue sustainable advance in social, cultural and other aims.

Note the idea of sustainability. We did prove ourselves able, before now, to deliver on social progress — but, we found, it was not of the enduring kind. Indeed, in years past the goose was plucked and its feathers handed out with abandon. In consequence, some geese winged their way to better climes. Others were rendered unproductive by those modern diseases — lack of competitiveness, and tax pressure.

Our touchstones in all we may do must be the concept of expanding sustainable employment at the fastest possible pace. This is the only solid foundation there can be for real progress in other respects. The requirements for employment must, therefore, remain uppermost in all our minds, whatever the task in hand. The kernel is to act so as to ensure a capacity for growth to existing domestic producers; and to show investors, domestic and foreign, that Ireland deserves major consideration when new enterprises are planned. How can we do this?

In fact it is not too difficult to distil the essence into a sentence or two! At one level, we must not only match, but outplay, the EC and the world at large on competitiveness. At another, we must demonstrate that investment in our economy is inherently less of a risk, and potentially more profitable, than investment elswhere.

As I see matters, the economic gurus tell us that we cannot reasonably expect to produce jobs enough for the exceptional expansion in the labour force over the next few years — at least not on the basis of the broad thrust of policy as we have known it. If they are believed we must anticipate significant emigration, or persistent high unemployment, into the earlier 1990s. The key business of this conference is to identify how we can upset the guru's expectations — be delivering more than they think possible!

I should preface my next remarks with one thought. I am not intent on setting out a statement of Government policy here — rather I am, so to speak, thinking aloud in the hope of getting some better answers. Let me, therefore, pose a few questions.

Let there be no doubt that our relatively unspoilt environment is a vital asset to this country. It enhances our image as an exporter of quality foods. It is an invaluable asset in tourism promotion. And let us not forget, it enhances the lives of our own people. But we must keep a proper balance in our approach. We can maintain standards and controls which give proper protection while affording industrial development decent opportunity to flourish.

We have long established practices in various areas of our society that, in effect, put certain categories in a position of privilege. Why, for example, do licences or permits to engage in a particular activity have a market price? I thought that permits only assumed an innate value in a protected market, which in turn must imply inflated prices for the services involved. Who is being protected? Is it really the customer? Who is bearing the cost? Is 'doing our best' for the job-seekers and the unemployed consistent with granting such privilege?

Should professionals predominate in their own 'regulatory' bodies, as they do among those structured under the law as well as on those arranged less formally? Is there just a smack of privilege here, at least in the area of dealing with complaints if not otherwise? More to the point, is there not something contradictory between the preference for 'free enterprise' expressed by many professionals, and the effective abolition of price-competition inherent in prescribing fee norms?

Can that do other than to raise the prices the rest of us have to pay for such services, feed inflation, and hurt our trade, growth and employment prospects in the process? Have they, and we, a still greater obligation — to end practices which inevitably, though circuitously, prompt emigration?

And what about 'safety nets' which the State puts in place with the aim of cushioning business from misfortune? The joint inability of management and worker to maintain competitiveness, which led to so many closures and redundancies, provoked a burden on the rest of enterprise. The Redundancy Fund was financed from the incomes of those who insisted on getting on successfully with their business, and faced the fact that pay or profit increases could not be afforded.

In the same vein, let me come to my audience here. Few of us can be oblivious of the sums poured into various 'commercial' State enterprises over the years. To what end? Certainly, to enable you to keep up with the demands of the market, and even set profit-making activity in train. But how often has the initial aid been provided only for recipients to return, seeking 'more'?

And what about the 'protective clothing' sometimes provided to sectors, firms, or sections of the labour force, when they claim to be 'under threat'? Is it not often the case that the threat comes from those who could, if allowed, provide the service cheaper and better? And wouldn't that, in turn, ease the task of survival for managements and workers who must live daily with the harsh realities of the international market-place?

At the global level, we acknowledge the merits of 'free trade' and the irrationality of protectionism; what is wrong with free trade within this economy? Should we be surprised if some, shielded by protective traditions, abuse the trust and leniency of society — by seeking to extract higher profits and better wages than the rest of us? Perhaps the 'Single Market' will do us all a favour if it removes the opportunity, and the inevitable temptation, to put the welfare of the vocal few ahead of the jobs of the silent majority!

Coming back to my own particular bailiwick — Finance — I am quite clear that advance to prosperity and growth in jobs in the 1990's is intimately bound up with progress in tax reform, as much as in overcoming our inheritance of debt. We could move steadily forward in the atmosphere of a tax system that provokes enterprise, rewards effort, favours thrift over consumption, and induces investment in growth!

In any restructuring of the tax system, there are winners and losers in the short term. The whole point, of course, is to direct incentives so as to make longer-term winners of us all!

Looking to 'your own small patch' one reality is that — excepting the commercial State entities, perhaps — we all exist 'on the public purse'. Your efficiency or otherwise impacts , in considerable measure, on producer-competitiveness via the tax burden which is necessary to the public sector's very existence. Your goals, like those of Robert McNamara, the Secretary for Defence in the US in the 1960s, include that of 'getting a bigger bang from each buck'. How many of you can put a hand on your hearts and assert that your 'operation', whatever it may be, is now more efficiently run than last year?

One often hears the slogan 'let the managers manage' as a recipe for improving efficiency. I think there is a great deal in this and, as I announced in this year's Budget, I have already taken steps to implement such a strategy in the Civil Service. This involves introducing a system to allow departments greater flexibility in running their own operations, within an agreed three-year budget cycle. Detailed negotiations are in progress with the Departments of Social Welfare and Energy and the Revenue Commissioners with a view to bringing the new system on stream in 1990.

I am glad to say that discussions will shortly commence with two other departments, Health, and Industry and Commerce, which have expressed particular interest in participating in this new and radical approach to running the civil service more efficiently.

I believe we have evolved, together, a leaner and fitter State sector since the sea-change in policy of 1987. But not to the point of complacency — I don't think any here would yet claim perfection, for example in the management of the 15% or so of GNP now devoted to public sector pay. A first challenge for you in the 1990s, therefore, is to continue the process of efficiency gain already initiated.

As to the commercial State sector, there can be only one, simple message. Those of you who provide inputs to internationally-trading producer and service entities must support and enhance their competitiveness. Unless your prices match — or better — the cost abroad of energy, communications, transport or whatever, you impose a disadvantage on domestic producers. Those of you who produce tradeable products know, more directly, that survival and expansion depend vitally on keeping one step ahead of the competition.

There is a further — and perhaps more important issue you might consider. The historic agreement by all the social partners in the Programme for National Recovery has served this country well. We must maintain that sense of common purpose. It is not enough, I think, that you and I be able to evolve, 'the right' policies. No strategy is worth the paper it's written on, unless it can be implemented. I have mentioned some potential areas of conflict between objectives — areas where, whichever way we jump, there are bound to be some who perceive themselves as losing out.

Our roles extend, in my view, beyond the tasks of working out, and deciding upon, the optimum policies. We must, in addition, make ourselves much more capable of selling those policies, on their real merits, to the nation. There is a need, I think, for all in the public domain — and here I unambiguously include all public servants — to recognise 'public education' as part of their function.

There is a tendency, too to defend the status quo, because of a view that to do otherwise would be to admit to error. Would it not be the greater error to maintain the ineffective, the wasteful or the unduly costly? In any event, can't altered circumstances often imply need for change in hitherto sensible policies?

My final challenge for the 1990s policy adviser is to 'get with it', to get involved in more fully assessing, and in informing the public mind, of the realities and the truths. Give us Ministers a better basis to bring the public to a more complete understanding of trade-offs; of the link from spending to taxation; of the conflict between short and longer term aspirations; and of the notion of schemes and programmes becoming out-dated.

WALTER GRÜNSTEIDL

# 1992 - A Challenge for Industry

THE other day somebody told me a parable to the effect that: 'A lion waking in the morning has one fundamental problem for the day. He must be faster than the slowest gazelle! Similarly a gazelle waking in the morning has one fundamental problem for the day. He must be faster than the fastest lion.' In some ways this reflects the kind of common problem of survival which we all face. I am talking here as a representative of a rather large company and I am not therefore talking specifically about Ireland. I would suggest however that most of what I say holds for all of us, all the industries and all the communities in our different European nations.

In terms of talking about challenges, a friend of mine told me the other day that one of the biggest deficiencies which we have developed is that we have stopped wondering - we are not easy to surprise any more. This whole avalanche of information, which affects us all, has apparently paralysed our senses. I believe that this is really true. We do not really appreciate what is going on in the world, and we fail to fully comprehend the incredibly dynamic evolution we are witnessing. You can be sure tomorrow when you read the newspaper that something dramatic has happened again. Just to illustrate this point, a week ago our total concept of how Europe could look has changed. The speech made by Mr. Gorbachev in Helsinki was critical in forcing us to look for a new definition of Europe as an economic entity. I think these are factors that we must now accommodate. What does this mean for us - what does it mean for those of us in politics, in business and indeed for society at large? It means that, when we talk about challenges for industry, the biggest challenge that I can see is that we have to create organisations and planning systems that are capable of responding to very unexpected and quite unpredictable change. We must find such adaptability, especially those of us in Europe who are also attempting to fulfil our obligations to create the European Single Market. We must learn to adapt to the new possibilities and opportunities which are prompted by the new economic reality in Europe.

I would like to outline some of the challenges which I believe industry now faces. I must also stress that in creating Europe 1992 we are only playing part of a bigger game, which involves us in the whole concept of a society in transition. This is a fundamental transition from what formerly was called the 'industrial society' to what is now called the 'information society'. I am not sure if this is a very good term, but it does reflect a new form of society characterised by the growth of complexity and interdependence. We must therefore find new solutions to this complexity. In industrial terms, this means new types of customers, new relationships with our employees where hierarchies start to crumble, and of course new competitors who must be reckoned with. Above all it means a radical change in corporate culture. As we participate in our own uniquely European development we must not lose sight of such global phenomena, and in particular the emergence of the global market place. We now have competitors at our doorstep of whom we knew nothing at all, only a short time ago. For example, in industrial terms there were no Japanese in the 1940s or 1950s. It would be foolish to similarly underestimate the current progress of the South Koreans and the Chinese. The phenomenon of global competition therefore requires the development of global strategies.

Research and development costs are soaring and involve ever increasing amounts of money, which invariably seem to reach the billions of dollars' range. For example, developing a new telephone switch costs in the region of one billion dollars; developing a new car, one billion dollars; developing the next generation of micro-chip, one billion dollars. Simultaneously, however, we find that this cost escalation is becoming associated with a pattern of ever shorter life-cycles, which means of course that the recovery of the initial costs becomes quite difficult and in some cases even impossible. As a result we find that industry is fighting this issue with all kinds of alliances and all kinds of practices. For example, dumping is essentially an attempt to get market share in order to recoup some losses later on.

Automation is now changing the industrial landscape and is giving rise to different notions of economy of scale. Maybe we will even replace the notion of economy of scale with the idea of economical flexibility which means that we can now work much closer to the customer. Automation will even change the trade patterns in the world because we do not need to shift products around any longer. We can sell closer to the customer because we can produce at the same level of costs almost everywhere in the world. On top of this, European industry faces some additional challenges which are specific to our European situation. The first is, of course, that we are now preparing for the new Single Market situation by re-structuring our industries. We are certainly very late in doing this. Why are we late? - because our politicians have consistently failed us for about thirty years since the signing of the Treaty of Rome. Politicians have failed to fulfil the promises they made in signing the treaty. The first blueprint for the creation of the Single Market came only in 1985 with the White Paper of Lord Cockfield. This has prompted us to do only now what we should have done much earlier and what our competitors elsewhere in the world have been doing for the last decades: that is to create the economies of scale which are needed to fight this global competitive struggle.

Another issue which we must address is that we, in Europe, have to cover higher costs. We must realise that in Europe, we have achieved something which is unique in the world. Nobody else has achieved the creation of economic growth and the consequent gradual increase in prosperity and employment (notwithstanding the very real size of the current unemployment problem). We have created high quality jobs in Europe. We have a vigorous industry and we have managed to develop it over the last few decades in parallel with a system of social justice and social security. On top of this we enjoy the luxury of investing heavily in public services' infrastructure for the public good. However, this means that we have to cover higher costs than our competitors in the rest of the world. This in turn means that if we want to improve and develop our social system further (and nobody wants to get rid of it), we will have to correct some of the inefficiencies of the past. The really great challenge for Europe and for European industry, is that we must secure our competitiveness without having to accept reductions in our social achievements and quality of life. We do not, however, want to turn Europe into a protectionist island. European industries must achieve a higher level of productivity than their best competitors from socially less developed countries, and this is the basic issue to be discussed with employees and unions in the future. The achievement of this objective lies at the heart of European well-being.

Europeans must also face another unique challenge. We must face the fact that some of us (e.g. the electronics and car industries) are targeted for termination by other economic blocs and industrial conglomerates elsewhere in the world. We must realise that our very survival is nowadays a central issue for us. The recent history of the European camera and watch industries offers a startling lesson in how survival cannot be taken for granted. Despite the fact that SWATCH has done a magnificent job in coming back and indeed this is a model example of how to fight such a situation, nevertheless the recent decline of both these industries illustrates the manner in which they were vulnerable to a targeted termination. You could say 'well, does this matter? Is it actually wrong? And anyway if you are weak you have to go'. In answer, however, we must enquire into the way in which such industrial termination has been brought about. We must, for example, identify the protectionist tendencies exhibited by our commercial enemy, and we must make it clear that we are prevented from enjoying the reciprocal advantage of entering his market or trading or investing in his country. If this pattern of trade is allowed to continue then the threat is of course more all-embracing. It is not only a question of jobs in the camera and watch industries. We will face a worsening trade deficit across all sectors, as is already the case with the electronic, computer and semi-conductor industries. Equally important, of course, is the fact that if this decline continues there will be a loss of skills in numerous support industries. The fact that there is no camera industry left in Europe means that if Philips should decide tomorrow to build a Cam-corder factory in Europe, we would not be able to purchase any lenses within Europe. This industry has gone. There is a professional lens industry but the main mass-produced lenses are not manufactured anymore in Europe. We cannot buy micro-motors anymore in Europe. We cannot buy recording heads any more in Europe. This has also affected the Americans, who now find that they cannot buy domestically certain types of memory chips. And what does all this mean? It means the loss of skills, the loss of R & D capacity and of course the stimulants for R & D. It also has an impact on the education system. As a small illustration of this, the closure of the textile industry in Northern Holland was followed two years later by the closure of the textile schools. We should understand, therefore, that this kind of process has a domino effect throughout the whole economic structure.

One possible answer to these threats (or to these challenges as I would call them) is that we have to make more use of the appropriate technology. The industrial society had its adequate technology in steam, coal and so on, and in the application of mechanical power. Nowadays our adequate technology is an information technology. We must make more use of it in our education systems, in our manufacturing processes, and in our service industries. The answer to these global developments lies in building a global strategy. We must be present in the industrialised areas of the world in an integrated way. That means not alone selling and not alone producing. Rather it implies the totality of the process, from development to production, and not just setting up what might be called 'screwdriver factories'. We in Europe, therefore, must foster strategic partnerships so as to gain market access, to pool knowhow, and to share risks. It is important that we should develop industrial policy with the very close co-operation of the political system, and in doing so we should attempt to create a much wider enthusiasm for the concept of 'centres of excellence'. We must also learn to use the negotiating power which we are now creating in a Single European Market and force the rest of the world to open up their fortresses. There is no fortress Europe but there is a fortress Japan; there is a fortress South Korea and shortly we will be faced with a fortress USA, because this protectionist trend is setting in more and more in America since they discovered that they have a severe technology gap.

So, this is the programme for industry, and it holds true for all of us, big or small. This global struggle leaves nobody alone — it is a struggle and a battle to be fought by all of us. We should now enter into a discussion with government for the development of joint action programmes. European industry has lost about thirty years in terms of preparing itself for the competitive struggle of the global market place. We must now join with government in finding ways to regain the initiative and to develop the policies for increasing our competitiveness. That means that together we must talk about programmes for stimulating market growth as part of a joint industrial policy programme. Such joint programmes, however, must be characterised by genuine pan-European participation, and should be based upon Euro-wide networks of information exchange. These are the only realistic programmes to provoke market growth, and to involve entrepreneurs in a structured joint action with government so as to help industry regain its technological edge. Creating healthy market conditions means fighting for trade reciprocity, but it also means highlighting the importance of R&D expenditures which should form such an essential feature of any joint action programme between government and industry. We must focus particularly on the small and medium-sized enterprises and we must offer appropriate support as they attempt to cope with the new conditions of the internal market and also with the pressures of the international market-place. Re-training programmes, for example, help to increase flexibility and adaptability, and we should particularly avoid taking any bureaucratic measures which might damage such adaptability and which in turn therefore could inhibit the operational freedom of entrepreneurs and companies. In addition we must devise together new training programmes for management development which will accentuate the need for product and service quality. I think we also need to develop a much greater involvement of entrepreneurs and industrialists directly in the political process. This is something which we have tended to ignore in Europe, although we in Philips are rather proud of the fact that it was an action plan drafted by a former Philips President in 1985 which acted as the catalyst for Lord Cockfield's White Paper. Indeed in recent years we have seen the beginning of a constructive debate between European politicians, national politicians and industrialists, and this is a trend which we need to expand and develop even further. Perhaps the reason why we have been slow to develop this type of dialogue is that in the past it may have been construed as 'lobbying' with all the negative connotations that that implies. Such negative perceptions, however reflect perhaps a rather American concept of the process, and we must therefore break away from such images and promote a constructive dialogue between politicians and industry. European politicians, parliamentarians, and the Commission, are more and more requested to take positions on technical issues of which they cannot possibly be expected to have a deep understanding. For example, it may be a question of a new satellite transmission system and the implications of its development within Europe. Industry therefore must offer its expertise in order to outline the key issues involved, and assist in the decision-taking process.

By way of conclusion, I would like to offer a brief resumé of my thoughts. We live in a world which is experiencing a fascinating period of change. This of course seems like a rather trite comment. Still, as trivial as it is, we would do well to reflect upon it. The situation in Europe is now changing almost daily, and this carries with it enormous implications for the manner in which we attempt to create prosperity and policy. We need now, more than ever before, to speed up the process of European integration and in particular to speed up the programme of the Single Market implementation. I agree very much with Chancellor Kohl's comment that the current dramatic changes in Eastern Europe would not have happened if we in the EC had not combined to address this enormous challenge, and to develop this vision of a Europe of the future where our young people could enjoy an even greater standard of living and an improved quality of life.

Finally I would like to offer some comments on the prospects for Ireland. I said at the outset that I would not be so presumptuous as to deal with Irish questions, but coming as I do originally from Austria, a country which has almost the same kind of problems as Ireland in that we both exist on the periphery of European developments, I feel that I can understand something of the Irish experience. Austria is also faced with the problem of a brain-drain; of producing too many talented people. Indeed exporting people is one of the major features of Austrian export activity, and I understand the same is true in Ireland. I believe, however, that it is now time for these small countries to go and develop further the concept of 'centres of excellence'. If we cannot identify a natural excellence (as for example in services like tourism, or special skills and talents of people to be applied in certain industrial activities) then we must agressively create and exploit such an excellence, so as to find a proper place in this concert of European countries. Once again this is something which can only be done within the context of a close partnership between industry and government. The Europe of the future will not be anything like the United States of America. We will always draw strength from the fact that we will be a conglomerate of norms, values, habits, languages, and to some extent, culture (although there is also something like a common European culture). Every nation will have to contribute to this process in their own way, so that we will achieve this rich mixture which forms the basis of our mental flexibility and creativity. On that we must capitalise. This, I would suggest, is the important message for all of us, and as such it is of course a message also for Ireland.

ALAN McCARTHY

# Economic Development in the 1990s — Some Views on Policy Directions

IRELAND is facing an uncertain outlook for economic development in the 1990s. There are a number of very positive indicators, and there is a consensus that Ireland will face a pattern of buoyant economic growth and a continuing improvement in the public finances over the next five years. Yet there is also a great uncertainty and a belief that the creation of an internal market in Europe will result in significant threats for a small peripheral country such as Ireland. The recent NESC report[1] argued that threats for manufacturing industry exist wherever manufacturing in Ireland is vulnerable to competition based on scale economies, or to intensive competition based on innovation. What I propose to consider today is where the opportunities are for economic development in the 1990s, and what the implications are for policy directions.

According to Peter Drucker the US expert on corporate economics, the 1990s will bring far reaching marketing changes. These changes will include the trend for businesses to 'integrate themselves into the world economy through alliances: minority participations, joint ventures, research and marketing consortia... and so on'[2]. One of the reasons for this rapidly accelerating trend is the fact that 'many middle-sized and even small businesses will have to become active in the world economy'[3]. These and other developments in the international market place would indicate a need to re-position Ireland's development priorities to focus on three areas as follows:

1. quality consumer products and services which reflect Ireland's comparative advantages;
2. firms meeting the sub-supply requirements of EC high technology industries; and
3. specialist niche market suppliers.

Before I outline my views on these issues, I would like to suggest a new policy perspective on the indigenous versus foreign industry debate.

**Indigenous versus foreign industry**

In considering the policy directions for Irish economic development in the 90s, one issue which is relevant relates to the question of indigenous versus foreign industry. Three aspects of this debate are of concern. Firstly, perceptions regarding the performance of indigenous firms versus foreign companies, secondly, the question of a rigid classification of indigenous companies, and thirdly the merits of overseas investment by indigenous firms. There is a mistaken view that Ireland's impressive export performance has been exclusively due to the exports of Ireland's foreign owned sector and that these exports contribute little in terms of value added remaining in the Irish economy. This depends on the import content of exports and the percentage of increased exports being repatriated as profits. These factors, of course, tend to differ for multinational foreign companies and for indigenous exporting firms. Despite this fact, the contribution of multinational firms to the value added resulting from exports remains of major significance to the Irish economy. There is, however, increasing awareness of the need to focus attention on the potential to develop exports from indigenous firms. Despite some opinions to the contrary, the indigenous sector has recorded a strong export performance in the past two years. There is a myth that the overall impressive export performance is only from the foreign owned sector, but in 1989 indigenous industry will again show significant export growth by historical standards.

An indication of the impressive performance of indigenous exports is provided by the results of a CTT/ESRI survey. In 1988 exports from these companies increased by 23% to reach £2.65 billion, and these firms had added 4,400 jobs at the end of 1988 compared to 1987. Strong export growth is reported by these firms in 1989 and exports increased by 15% in the first half of the year.

It is clear that the overall export growth has in recent years been broadly based and this is also reflected in the sectoral performance of exports. An indication of this factor is highlighted in Table 1. The data show that only a tiny percentage of exports declined over the period and that for the vast majority of sectors a significant growth in exports was achieved. Most of the sectors where exports declined were in commodity areas, for example live animals, petroleum and related materials, etc. Overall the data encouragingly highlights the fact that the export growth during the first half of 1989 was broadly based.

Table 1: **Sectoral performance of exports January - June 1989**

| | Sectors where exports declined | Sectors where growth was below 17.4% | Sectors where export growth exceeded 17.4% and below 29% | Sectors where export growth exceeded 29% |
|---|---|---|---|---|
| % of exports | 3.2 | 23.9 | 26.3 | 46.6 |

*Source:* CSO/CTT

On the question of indigenous versus foreign companies, I also believe it would be a mistake to take too rigid a definition of indigenous industry, and that it would in particular be a mistake to focus exclusively on the issue of ownership. The key issue should rather relate to the extent to which the project is a stand-alone integrated operation whose success depends on its performance in Ireland. Organisations where marketing, strategic management and other key business functions are located in the Irish company, where sales are not simply to affiliates and which have high value added, are very different from foreign owned mobile assembly type operations where all key decisions are made overseas.

I realise that if one moves away from exclusive attention on ownership it certainly makes a classification more difficult, but the focus must be on a judgement concerning the nature of the operation and not simply on ownership.

To illustrate the force of this argument it is useful to consider the examples of Irish Biscuits and Essco Collins. If a rigid Irish ownership criteria was used, none of these companies would be considered as indigenous companies. The ownership of the W & R Jacob Group, which was founded in 1851, has been continuously changing. In 1966 the biscuit interests of Bolands Ltd were purchased and merged with Jacobs into a subsidiary company called Irish Biscuits. Irish Biscuits is one of a number of companies owned by W & R Jacob Plc. The Nabisco Group up to this year held 29.7% share interest in the firm. This was subsequently sold to BSN Group earlier this year. Twenty-five per cent of Irish Biscuits production is exported. The company produces a range of sixty products, twenty of which are sold and exported under the Bolands name. Turnover in 1988 was £45.7m. The company's main export markets are UK, Netherlands, Spain, France, US and Canada. All the firm's management and marketing is located in Tallaght.

Essco Collins Ltd is a joint venture between Collins Steelplejacks, a long established Clare-based company, and Essco Corporation, USA manufacturers of environmental protective coverings for radar and antennae systems. The joint venture was established in 1975 as the European manufacturing base of Essco Corp. The Irish company now handles most non USA markets including China, Europe, Middle East and Australia. Essco Collins employs forty persons in a remote location in Co. Clare and, with marketing control for its production now based in Ireland, is perceived as an indigenous company. All management and staff are Irish.

The issue of classification of indigenous versus foreign is not an academic question as it has implications for the provision of State support services. A classification based solely on ownership is no longer adequate and must be amended if we are to achieve Ireland's economic development potential in the 1990s.

The final issue regarding indigenous industry which requires re-examination relates to the merits of overseas investment by indigenous firms. In many cases the most promising Irish indigenous firms have been criticised for their overseas investment programmes. The answer to this is not to expect companies to ignore overseas investment opportunities but rather to create the conditions and incentives so that increased investment in Ireland will be the commercially appropriate decision. In some cases, however, success of the Irish entity may depend on overseas investment and in these cases such investment should be actively encouraged rather than frowned on. It is generally accepted that, in some sectors, overseas investment to purchase market share may be the only option available. For example, Danaher pointed out that in some industries 'where there are significant entry barriers', acquisitions or joint ventures may be the only feasible way to penetrate foreign markets'. Also in relation to indigenous industry, it is important to break the myth that indigenous firms are only in the traditional industry sectors such as clothing, food, furniture and footwear and that overseas companies are exclusively involved in the new high tech sectors. There are in fact many examples of the inverse of this myth, for example the multinational Rowntree Macintosh involvement in the confectionery sector in Ireland, and the indigenous firm Clonmel Chemicals, who are leaders in the manufacture of generic drugs and medicines for export markets.

While the 1990s will represent a threat to some sectors of Irish manufacturing, there will also be new opportunities. In evaluating the appropriate strategic positioning of Ireland's development priorities, it is essential that account is taken of developments in the international marketplace. These developments include increasing importance of market share as a competitive determinant in many sectors, EC-wide sourcing by high technology companies, success of high quality consumer goods manufacturers, and the trend towards marketing alliances as a means of penetrating overseas markets. The opportunities for Ireland presented by these market developments will in part depend on the image of Ireland and this is considered below.

**International perceptions of Ireland**

In considering the positioning of Ireland in the international marketplace, either from the perspective of trade in manufactured goods or in international services (such as tourism, or professional/financial services), it is useful to consider how Ireland is viewed from outside. Research on international perceptions of Ireland undertaken in 1988 by IMS indicated the views of a sample of populations in the United States, Great Britain and Germany. Ireland's natural assets as a country of beautiful scenery and rich, natural environment are the dominant attractions for Britons and Americans. Germans are probably among the most environmentally conscious populations in the world and almost four out of ten Germans perceive Ireland as a country of clean air and unpolluted rivers and seas, and see these qualities as one of the major attractions of Ireland.

Perceptions of national competence, as estimated by British people and by Germans, tend to reflect the perhaps somewhat idealised imagery attaching to Ireland as a country. Ireland has a very strong image in relation to anything associated with agriculture. Both Britons and Germans agree that Irish meat, dairy and vegetable products are likely to be of a high standard. We are also highly regarded in terms of competence in the area of producing alcoholic drinks, natural fabrics (like wool and tweed) and simple traditional handcrafts. Whereas the average Briton would commonly associate Ireland with a high degree of competence in the area of sophisticated handcrafts (such as crystal, porcelain or jewellery), this is not as widely accepted by Germans. The consumer research indicates the perception that the Irish would not be particularly competent at producing computers or other electronic products, machinery or high-grade fashion garments. Of course perceptions can be changed, but not as easily as may be first imagined.

**Export opportunities for high quality consumer goods manufacturers**

The perceptions of Ireland from the international marketplace highlight the comparative advantage which Ireland has in developing export sales in certain high-quality consumer goods areas. International market trends in the key EC countries indicate that many of these high-quality discretionary items of consumer expenditure are also growing rapidly. In some cases market trends such as the increasing commercial importance of environmental factors in purchasing decisions give added weight to the market perceptions of Ireland's comparative advantages. It would be a mistake to assume that Irish-based firms have not already developed high quality consumer goods to meet the opportunities which exist in Europe, and we are all familiar with the high profile stories such as Kerrygold's success in selling branded butter in Germany at premium prices and the international marketing success of products such as Baileys Cream Liqueur. I would, however, like to highlight an example from the food sector which may be less well-known but which highlights the opportunities which can be secured by Irish-based firms in this area, namely the example of Tipperary Spring Water. I would also like to mention an initiative taken by a major German retail organisation, which again highlights the real market opportunities for Irish-based firms supplying European quality consumer goods markets.

Tipperary Spring Water Co Ltd was established in 1986, part of the M & J Gleeson Group, which specialises in soft drinks production, and drinks wholesaleing. The company is the major exporter of Irish mineral water to the US. It has concentrated on the US market since the beginning and sells through Waters of Ireland, which distributes throughout the Tri-State area. It also sells into Europe, with special emphasis on the Belgian market, where it has had considerable success. Tipperary is in the process of considerable change at present, with the installation of a £4 million new plant at Borrisoleigh, and the appointment of additional marketing personnel to the company. A major onslaught on markets is planned for 1990, with particular emphasis on the US. The company continues to maintain a high level of advertising and promotional activities, and export markets. The company has a history of 'firsts' — it was the first Irish company to obtain the EC official Mineral Water status, which is a significant marketing advantage; and it was also the first company in Ireland to develop the water cooler business which is now a major part of its total business. Tipperary Spring Water is an example of an indigenous company that has focused on supplying branded high quality consumer goods to export markets. There are hundreds of other examples of Irish-based success stories in consumer goods, but the potential to develop additional export sales is effectively unlimited.

An example of a European initiative which capitalises on the perceptions of Ireland and the opportunities for high quality consumer goods is the initiative taken by the German Co-op Handels company, a subsidiary of the giant Co-op Holdings. This venture is an example of the value, in European eyes, of Ireland's reputation as a clean, green, unpolluted island, and the opportunities which exist to build on this perception of Ireland. In 1988 Peter Van Aart, then a director of the vast German Co-Op organisation, approached the Irish state agencies regarding his 'natur pur' project. Briefly, Co-Op was in the process of reorganising and upgrading its operations; Van Aart conceived the idea of getting together a collection of Irish food products and presenting them to the consumer as a totally new, top quality and healthy range, emphasising the Irish origins, and explaining why product from Ireland has such healthy positive attributes — island location on the periphery of Europe, washed by the clean Atlantic; small population, traditional farming methods, etc. The Irishness was connected with environmentally pure, healthy qualities; this would provide Co-Op with a different story, pitched at a suitable quality premium level and fitted nicely into the current concern with health and environment. The 'green' message was to be reinforced through the ideal vehicle — the green island. This initiative involved significant purchases of beef and lamb, poultry, mineral waters, muesli, fish products, dairy products, cream liqueur, and ready meals.

Ultimately, Van Aart located an Irish company to share in this project — Campbell International Trading, who have now become partners in the venture. In Spring 1989, a regional launch of the products was held in Munich and the plan was to roll out a series of launches by various regions. Initial reaction to the range was good, but internal difficulties within Co-Op developed throughout 1989. However, the concept is being developed by a new company involving Campbells and Van Aart.

**Export opportunities in the sub-supply sector**

Indigenous exporters of industrial products from Ireland must overcome the marketing obstacles which arise due to the perception that Ireland would not be particularly competent in this area. This problem does not of course apply in this form to multinational companies who base operations in Ireland selling to affiliate companies or utilising established world brand names. Exporters of industrial products from Ireland also face the fact that in many industrial sectors, such as electrical engineering, the completion of the EC internal market will intensify competition based on scale economies and product development. This combined with international technical and organisational changes will give rise to restructuring of many industrial sectors throughout Europe. Industry in Ireland will be vulnerable to these changes in the 1990s. The changes in the international marketplace impact on the behaviour of firms and increasing concentration and intensified competition is resulting in centralised, streamlined purchasing. An example from the automobile sector highlights this trend.

Increasingly, the motor companies are planning to have one central location for purchasing and production at plants throughout Europe which is controlled from this location. It is usually also the design centre. For one particular motor company, purchasing for its Belgian, UK and German factories is all done from Russelsheim outside Frankfurt. This is likely to result in a reduction in the number of sub suppliers used, but also will result in companies contracting out sub-supplies which were previously manufactured in-house. This will inevitably lead to a standardisation of components between different manufacturers. Once a company is accepted as a sub-supplier to a major electronics or automobile manufacturer this provides a basis for selling to other leading manufacturers in the same sector. Sub-suppliers acceptance can therefore act as a calling-card/recommendation to other leading purchasers. This referral system can assist suppliers from small countries such as Ireland to overcome the marketing obstacles to EC-wide sales.

These market developments which involve the rationalisation of major companies clearly present an opportunity for firms in Ireland who have succeeded in selling to multinationals based here or who have developed highly specialised technical skills. With rationalisation, companies are deciding to purchase in sub-supplies from more economic producers. If firms in Ireland achieve sufficient scale and quality standards the restructuring of European industry could provide very significant market opportunities for Irish-based firms to provide the sub-supply requirements of European industry. In particular, there are major opportunities in the electronics and automobile sectors. For illustrative purposes it is useful to consider examples from the Waterford/Wexford area of firms in Ireland which have already developed market opportunities supplying raw materials and components to EC industry. It is also useful to consider the results of a recent CTT initiative to assist sub-suppliers.

One example of an Irish-based company which is exploiting opportunities to meet sub-supply requirements of EC industry is the Waterford engineering company, Garrett Ireland Ltd. Garrett recently won Rolls Royce Aeroengines plc approval to begin production of compressor blades for Rolls Royce jet engines. The initial order, which was won with CTT assistance, now allows the company to work towards winning a potential £4 million in export sales to Rolls Royce over the next five years and gives the company a significant entrée into the lucrative international aircraft components market. It paves the way for further export sales and a major employment boost at the Waterford plant, which currently employs 297 people. The contract marks the first stage of Garret Ireland's bid to set up an independent export sales operation in Ireland. Previously the company was engaged solely in supplying components to its US parent, the giant $12 billion turnover Allied Signal conglomerate, which specialises in the manufacture of turbine engines for aircraft.

Also of interest is the example of Waterford Electronics (Smiths) which employs 400 in the manufacture of wiring harnesses for Renault 5, Renault Espace and JCB. This Irish-owned company employs an EDI system which is updated daily.

The potential which exists for Irish-based electronics/engineering and other sub-supply firms to supply the industrial sector in Britain and Continental Europe was also demonstrated by the CTT Source Ireland programme.The programme aims to raise the awareness of buyers in Holland, France, Germany and the UK of the range and quality of industrial components and sub-supplies produced in Ireland. The programme is aimed at over 470 identified key purchasing organisations and aims at obtaining business for 300 small and medium-sized firms based in Ireland. To date the reaction to the programme has been exceptional and we expect orders in excess of £45m to arise from the initiative in 1989 and £75m in 1990.

**Export opportunities in specialist niche markets**

While there are very significant disadvantages facing Irish-based companies in developing export markets in high volume mass-produced markets, these difficulties could be overcome if Irish companies were successful in obtaining a very high world market share in specialist niche markets. It is likely that the completion of the internal market will have a major impact on specialised niche market manufacturers. As the non-tariff barriers are removed the potential market sizes for niche suppliers will expand significantly. The possibility of exploiting niche markets is influenced by the conclusion identified by Drucker that many middle-sized and even small businesses will have to become active in the world economy. Drucker pointed out that 'to maintain leadership in one developed market, a company increasingly has to have a strong presence in all such markets worldwide'. There are a number of potential implications of this conclusion, including the option of marketing alliances or alternatively pursuing a niche market strategy.

Such a niche market strategy is essential in many sectors if Irish indigenous firms are to achieve a secure market share in the US and Japanese markets as well as in Continental Europe.

The difficulties in achieving high market share must not be underestimated, but it is useful to consider the Danish example. Denmark has succeeded in developing a large number of very specialised niche market players concentrating on export markets. It is useful to consider some examples and to compare these with the very small market shares held by Irish companies. In the hearing aids sector, the Danish company Danavox has approximately 70% of the world market. In acoustic engineering, Bruel and Kjaer has 60% of the market for ultrasonic electro-medical equipment. The Danish manufacturer Nordisk Ventilator, has installed ships' ventilators in 25% of the world's commercial fleet. In the manufacture of enzymes and insulin, Novo/Nordisk Gentofte has over 60% of the world market. Numerous other examples could also be provided by Danish companies in other niche markets such as weighing scales, ethnic food production, milk driers, food vending machines, etc.

A number of Irish firms are already pursuing the ambitious strategy of developing world market niches. One interesting example is Intepro Systems Ltd. This company manufactures automatic test equipment for testing power supplies. This is a specific market niche with very few other dedicated competitors. The company is market leader in Europe for this type of test equipment and has captured approximately 30% of the North American market. It is now making major inroads into the Far East where there is only one other significant competitor. The company concentrates on major original equipment manufacturing OEMs where it can get referrals. This results in carrying large upfront costs in getting the initial order but also results in subsequent lower costs per contract for referred orders. In addition, major OEMs are excellent credit risks. The major strategic step for the company was entering into a joint venture with a North American company (Elgar Corporation - Elgar Intepro). This gave Intepro imediate credibility with major OEMs and access to a national distribution network. The company was funded in penetrating the US market by the Med's Scheme and also participated in the Group Office Project in Boston. The company has direct marketing operations in the UK, US and a dedicated distributor in Germany.

Another interesting example of an Irish company with a highly focused marketing strategy in niche market areas is Kindle, the Irish international services company. Kindle was founded in 1978 and has developed into Ireland's largest own software company. Current employment is 303 people, 75 of whom are based in Ireland. Kindle's principle packaged product is called Bank Master. It initially ran only on ICL computers but has now been ported onto new systems. It is designed to manage banking operations and now has a customer base of approximately sixty banks in 200 sites worldwide.

Kindle's strategy has been to address two niche market segments: (a) Small retail banks in under-developed countries, and (b) Wholesale or mortgage companies in developed countries. The company has developed a strong position in the under-developed countries because of its close links with ICL who are one of the dominant hardware suppliers in these markets. It hopes to strengthen its position in these markets with the new release of Bank Master, which will run under a variety of new operating systems. While holding such a large market share has potential danger in terms of a downturn in demand, the market power associated with such market penetration provides the basis for sustained export successes.

**Policy implications**

I have argued that the creation of the EC internal market and other market developments in Europe will leave some Irish sectors vulnerable to competition but will also open up new opportunities for Ireland in three areas, namely producers of high-quality consumer goods and services, sub-supply producers, and industrial niche market players. This is not to suggest that only firms in these sectors will succeed or that Irish government agencies should attempt to introduce rigid guidelines on the sectors to obtain assistance. Individual entrepreneurs thankfully have a habit of making any generalised guidelines in this area appear inappropriate. Also, many multinational manufacturers may successfully locate in Ireland in areas which do not build on Ireland's comparative market advantages. It is, however, important to consider a market-led approach to allocating priorities to assist industrial development. Even within the three broad areas which I indicated from an analysis of overseas market opportunities and Ireland's strengths, it would not be possible to make a significant impact in all EC markets. What I believe is required is a more targeted approach focusing on specific regions of opportunity. New strategies to take account of this approach have recently been launched by CTT in European markets in 1989 and include the following:

1. A Regional Markets and Marketing Alliances Programme which will focus on growth regions in the EC, with the objective of identifying business opportunities and suitable marketing partnerships for Irish firms. In 1989, Catalonia, Lombardy and Denmark were the focus of this programme. The regional markets programme is targeted to secure an increase of £82m in exports in 1989 and £150m in exports in 1990.
2. A Source Ireland Programme focused on the UK and Germany, which will identify market leads for Irish firms and encourage foreign industrialists to source business in Ireland.
3. An Advancement Products Programme to help small firms adapt and improve products for EC markets.

There is, however, a need to consider a more ambitious effort to build on Ireland's market strengths on an integrated regional basis in EC countries. These would merit, initially on a pilot basis, targeting a region in Continental Europe and making a significant investment in marketing Ireland in the interests of Irish tourism and Irish quality consumer goods and services, as well as Irish sub-supply producers. While existing agencies of the Irish government are appropriately compartmentalised in terms of exports, inward investment, tourism, and foreign affairs, there is a case for taking a share of the budgets from all these important national tasks and implementing a marketing programme for Ireland on a regional basis. One of the merits of targeting a very specific region is that it is possible to monitor rigorously the impact of any such investment. Investment in marketing, needs as careful or indeed more careful evaluation as investment in plant and machinery. Appropriate marketing investment at either a national or company level can not only result in a significant return on expenditure but can indeed be the key determinant of economic or commercial success. Similarly, unresearched and badly-designed marketing expenditure can simply be a waste of very scarce resources. Some people believe that increasing the level of marketing budgets regardless of how they are spent is in itself the panacea for Ireland's economic difficulties. Others believe that marketing is a somewhat vague concept, distrust the value of marketing strategies and are sceptical about the return on any marketing expenditures. Both of these ill-informed attitudes must be abandoned once and for all by both public servants and private industry if Ireland's development effort is to succeed in the 1990s.

In conclusion, therefore, I believe we need to re-examine traditional beliefs regarding economic development and some of our views on issues such as the definition of indigenous companies will, I believe, not emerge unchanged from such a review. We need to decide on priorities for our industrialisation efforts on the basis of overseas market developments. We also need to target our resources in an integrated manner on specific areas of greatest opportunities. Government policy as well as decisions by the individual enterprises must be guided by a detailed assessment of research on the requirements of the international marketplace. I am confident that, despite the unprecedented structural change in markets and industry sectors which I expect in the 1990s sensible policy development would facilitate exporters to invest in appropriate product and market development and to secure new market opportunities in the enlarged EC market.

**Notes**

1. NESC Report etc.
2. Peter Drucker 1990s - The futures that have already happened, The Economist, October 21, 1989.
3. Drucker, op cit.
4. 'Responding to the challenges of 1992', Gerry Danaher, Secretary, NESC, Conference paper to the Irish Council of the Europen Movement, 2 October 1989.
5. Drucker, op cit.

HARTMUT FEST

# Employment and Labour Market Policies

THE subject of my presentation is inherently wider than the heading suggests, as labour market and employment performance are simultaneously determined by the interdependence of goods, capital and labour markets, all together interacting with macroeconomic developments. Hence, there is not an *a priori* presumption that employment and labour market policies, taken by themselves, are best suited to reduce high unemployment and correct malfunctioning labour markets. I have been asked to focus on some possible lessons for Ireland that might be drawn from other OECD countries' experience, in particular the smaller open economies. In this undertaking I shall proceed as follows.

First, I wish to summarise the principal features of Ireland's significant economic turnaround since 1987. The remaining imbalances are nonetheless large, and my comments are focused on the structural rigidities that are behind Ireland's high increase in unemployment. Secondly, I will review OECD countries comparative employment and labour market performance over the 1980s on the basis of a number of summary and institutional indicators meant to capture the key characteristics of labour-market efficiency.

I will discuss detailed measures of labour market structure and policy stance that provide evidence about relative success and failure of labour market institutions and policies. Finally, I will sketch out the main areas for further reform that may have a beneficial impact on Irish employment and labour market performance over the medium-term.

To provide a broader perspective on the subject matter, which is to identify desirable changes in respect of their labour market impact, it may be illuminating to recall the different paradigms which underlie the broad assessments that are inevitably present when we judge structural adjustment and the policies aimed at influencing it (Figure 1). Of the four graphs, which depict simplified relationships representing very complex realities, the bottom panel suggests opposite patterns of optimality. The left one, it appears, is intuitively more appealing to reason than the 'extremes-are-best' paradigm. Yet, it is the latter that is often found to be associated with labour market issues. I will substantiate this position in due course and turn now to Irish economic performance.

**The Multiple Theoretical Paradigms Underlying Different 'Indicators of Structural Policy'**

FIGURE 1

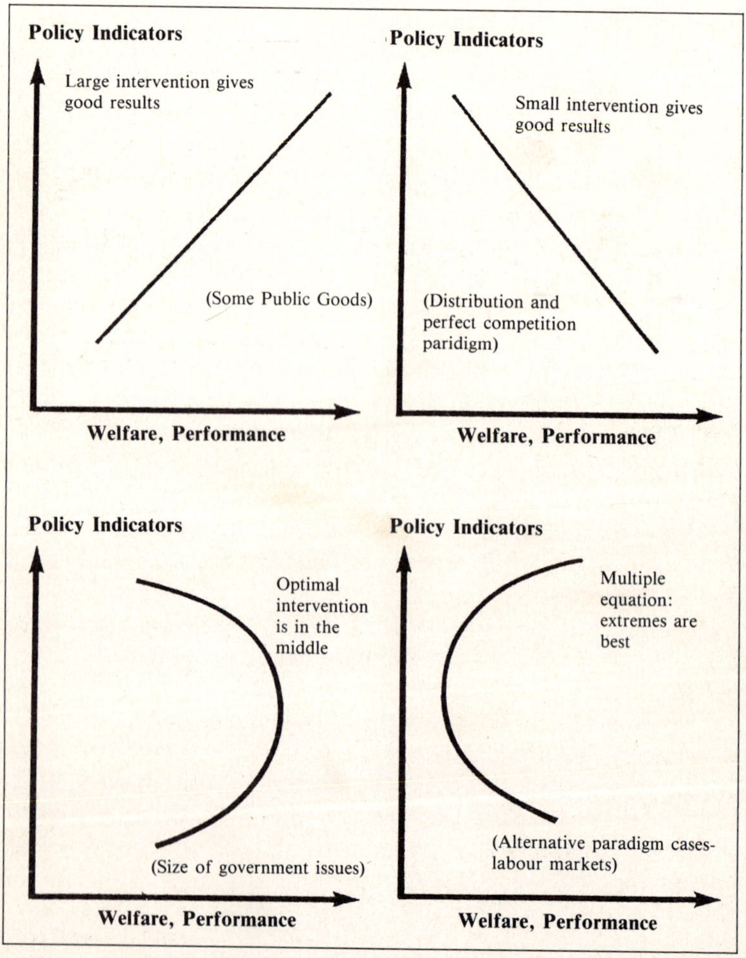

There has been a major improvement in Irish macroeconomic performance since 1987, mainly due to the combined effects of four factors: an effective appreciation of the Irish pound; a large fall in oil prices; a strong recovery of world trade; and a significant fiscal consolidation under the Programme for National Recovery, to be continued under the National Development Plan.

FIGURE 2

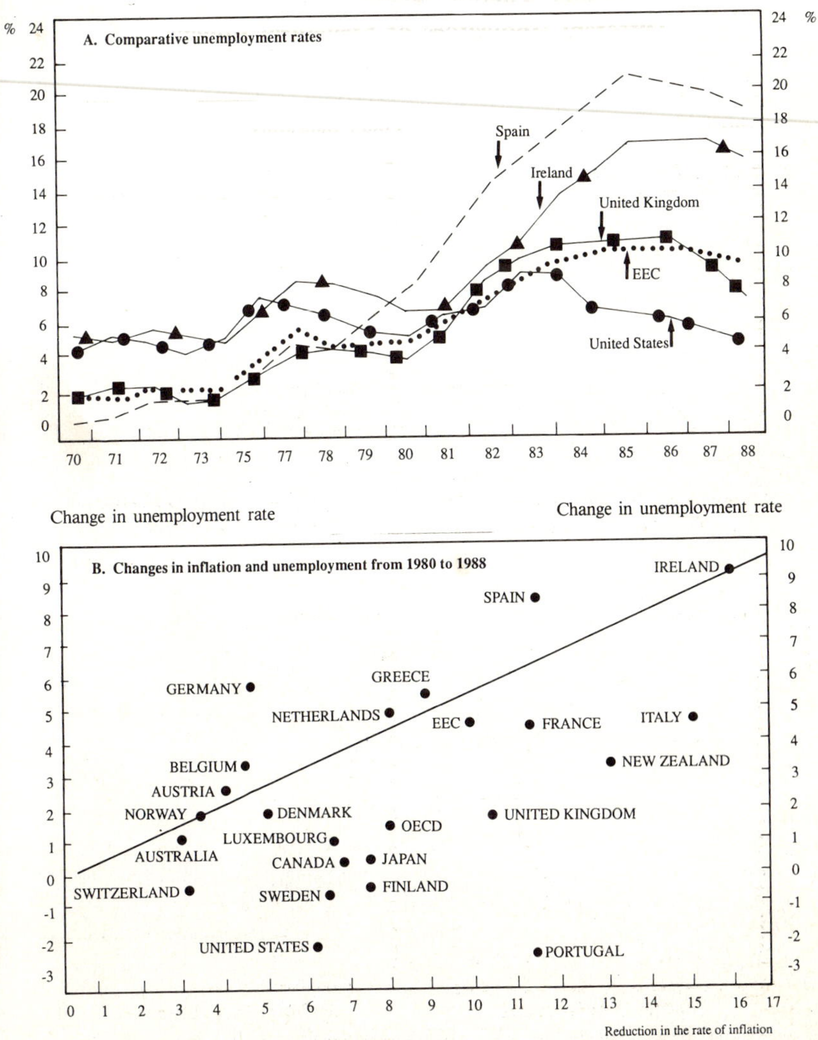

The net cumulative impact of these influencs was tantamount to an increase in the level of GNP of nearly one percentage point and a reduction in the domestic price level by almost six percentage points between 1986 and 1988. Hence, the significant turnaround witnessed by the Irish economy has been the result of both successful fiscal consolidation and highly favourable external developments.

Despite the marked improvement in macroeconomic performance, substantial structural problems remain relating to the external balance, unemployment, inflation and the budget balance (Figure 2). Between 1981 and 1986, the current external deficit shrank from 15 per cent of GNP to 4 per cent, and inflation fell from 20 to 4 per cent. The major factor contributing to the disinflation process has been the decline in unit wage costs. High and increasing labour market slack, the change of wage determination from a system of centrally-negotiated wages in the 1970s and early 1980s to decentralised bargaining, and incomes policy under the Programme for National Recovery, are all likely to have contributed to the observed reduction in labour cost pressure. Ireland has achieved the largest reduction in inflation in the OECD area from 1980 to 1988.

On the other hand, unemployment rose rapidly from 10 to 17 per cent of the labour force, with the speed of the increase and the level of Ireland's unemployment rate higher than elsewhere, except for Spain. The increase in the unemployment rate from 1980 to 1988 was the largest in the OECD area, despite large net emigration and a decline in the participation rate. Rising unemployment has been characterised by an increasing proportion of long-term unemployed. Those who have been out of work for more than 53 weeks accounted for about 45 per cent of total unemployment, while slightly over one-quarter of the total unemployed were under 25 years of age in 1988. The level of employment last year was still six per cent below the level in 1980.

The experience of unemployment has been common to most OECD economies since the first oil price shock (Table 1). The unemployment rate in the OECD area, which rose every year since 1973 (except 1978 and 1979), peaked in 1983 at 9 per cent. Since then, it has fallen slowly each year to about 1½ per cent in 1988. Behind this overall performance lie sharp differences in individual country experiences. How far can labour market functioning explain the important differences between countries?

## able 1: Growth and labour market performance

### Average annual growth rates

| | GDP | | Employment | | Labour force | | Change in participation rates | | Unemployment rate | | |
|---|---|---|---|---|---|---|---|---|---|---|---|
| | 1973-83 | 1983-88 | 1973-83 | 1983-88 | 1973-83 | 1983-88 | 1973-83 | 1983-88 | 1973 | 1983 | 1988 |
| ited States | 1.8 | 4.0 | 1.7 | 2.7 | 2.2 | 1.8 | 0.7 | 0.8 | 4.9 | 9.6 | 5.5 |
| anada | 3.0 | 4.5 | 2.1 | 2.9 | 2.8 | 2.0 | 0.9 | 1.0 | 5.5 | 11.9 | 7.8 |
| pan | 3.6 | 4.5 | 0.9 | 1.0 | 1.0 | 0.9 | 0.2 | −0.3 | 1.3 | 2.7 | 2.5 |
| ance | 2.3 | 2.2 | 0.1 | −0.1 | 0.8 | 0.3 | −0.2 | −0.3 | 2.7 | 8.4 | 10.3 |
| ermany | 1.6 | 2.6 | −0.6 | 0.6 | 0.1 | 0.6 | −0.6 | 0.2 | 1.0 | 8.2 | 7.9 |
| aly | 2.2 | 3.2 | 0.7 | 0.6 | 1.1 | 1.1 | 0.2 | 0.2 | 5.9 | 9.2 | 11.1 |
| nited Kingdom | 1.0 | 3.5 | −0.5 | 1.7 | 0.4 | 1.1 | −0.1 | 1.0 | 2.1 | 11.2 | 8.5 |
| ustria | 2.4 | 2.0 | 0.1 | 0.5 | 0.4 | 0.5 | −0.3 | −0.1 | 0.9 | 3.7 | 3.7 |
| elgium | 1.8 | 2.1 | −0.4 | 0.6 | 0.7 | — | 0.1 | −0.3 | 2.3 | 12.9 | 10.5 |
| enmark | 1.5 | 2.1 | 0.1 | 1.6 | 1.1 | 1.2 | 0.7 | 0.6 | 1.0 | 10.4 | 8.5 |
| inland | 2.8 | 3.4 | 0.5 | 0.4 | 0.9 | 0.2 | 0.8 | 0.1 | 2.5 | 5.4 | 4.7 |
| eland | 2.5 | 1.4 | 0.5 | −0.7 | 1.5 | −0.1 | −0.1 | −0.7 | 5.7 | 14.0 | 16.6 |
| etherlands | 1.9 | 2.3 | −0.4 | 1.1 | 1.0 | 0.5 | 0.3 | −0.5 | 3.1 | 15.0 | 12.5 |
| orway | 3.9 | 3.3 | 1.6 | 1.7 | 1.8 | 1.6 | 1.2 | 1.2 | 1.6 | 3.4 | 3.1 |
| ortugal | 2.6 | 2.9 | 2.1 | 0.8 | 2.7 | 0.5 | 1.0 | −1.8 | 2.2 | 7.9 | 6.5 |
| pain | 1.9 | 3.6 | −1.4 | 1.1 | 0.4 | 1.4 | −0.8 | −0.2 | 2.2 | 18.2 | 19.5 |
| weden | 1.5 | 2.4 | 0.8 | 0.7 | 0.9 | 0.4 | 0.7 | — | 2.0 | 2.9 | 1.7 |
| witzerland | 0.3 | 2.7 | −0.4 | 0.9 | −0.3 | 0.9 | −0.8 | −0.1 | — | 0.8 | 0.7 |
| Australia | 2.1 | 4.2 | 0.8 | 3.1 | 1.6 | 2.5 | — | 0.8 | 2.3 | 9.9 | 7.4 |
| New Zealand | 0.9 | 1.8 | 1.1 | 0.8 | 1.6 | 0.8 | 0.1 | 4.8 | 0.2 | 5.4 | 5.3 |
| Total OECD | 2.1 | 4.2 | 0.7 | 1.6 | 1.3 | 1.2 | 0.2 | 0.4 | 3.5 | 8.9 | 7.4 |
| OECD Europe[1] | 1.8 | 4.2 | — | 0.9 | 0.8 | 0.8 | −0.1 | 0.1 | 3.5 | 10.4 | 10.3 |
| *Of which:* | | | | | | | | | | | |
| Low unemployment countries[2] | 2.1 | 2.8 | 0.4 | 0.8 | 0.6 | 0.7 | 0.2 | 0.1 | 1.3 | 3.1 | 2.6 |
| High unemployment countries[3] | 1.7 | 2.8 | −0.2 | 0.8 | 0.7 | 0.8 | −0.2 | 0.1 | 2.7 | 10.6 | 10.6 |
| Low unemployment countries[4] | 2.2 | 4.1 | 1.4 | 2.0 | 1.8 | 1.4 | 0.5 | 0.5 | 3.4 | 7.2 | 4.6 |

*Note:* Percentage changes (or rates) for groups of countries are the percentage changes (or the ratios) of the aggregate series for the group. GDP aggregates are expressed in US dollars at constant exchange rates.

1. Excluding Greece, Turkey, Yugoslavia.
2. Austria, Finland, Norway, Sweden, Switzerland.
3. Germany, France, United Kingdom, Italy, Belgium, Denmark, Netherlands, Portugal, Spain.
4. Countries listed in (2) above plus United States, Japan and Canada.

*Sources:* OECD, *Economic Outlook, Historical Statistics, 1960-1987.* Estimates for 1988 are from *Economic Outlook* 44 (December 1988).

Countries can be divided into three broad groups:

1. In the first group unemployment rates have been brought down almost to their pre-OPEC I levels: the United States, Canada, Japan, and some European countries (Austria, Finland, Norway, Sweden and Switzerland) are all in this category. In this group, as a whole, the unemployment rate had, by 1988, fallen to 4.6 per cent, only a little higher than in 1973 (shown in the final line of Table 1). Note that this group comprises two kinds of countries, with sharply different labour market institutions.

2. In a second group unemployment was, by 1988, still close to its peak rate. This included most European countries (the major four plus Belgium, Denmark, Ireland, the Netherlands, Portugal and Spain). The average unemployment rate rose sharply from 1973 to 1983, and has fallen only a little since then. By 1988, it was more than twice as high as in the first group.

3. Australia and New Zealand are in a third group: unemployment has remained much higher than at the beginning of the 1970s, but not as high as in the second group of European countries.

Uneven rates of unemployment across countries may reflect, in part, different growth of output as well as other factors. Economic growth has been faster, on average in low-unemployment countries than in medium and high unemployment countries. The largest increases in employment from 1983 to 1988 occurred in the United States, Canada and Australia - all countries where annual growth in GDP was around four per cent or more. The labour intensity of growth also differed considerably among countries. Expansion appears to have been most labour-intensive in North America. European countries in general experienced much lower employment growth than non-European countries. For most of the countries in the high-unemployment European group, employment in 1988 was still below the level last attained in 1973; the notable exceptions were Italy and Portugal. Countries with the strongest employment growth have also experienced the fastest increase in the supply of labour in the last fifteen years. The labour force in the United States, Canada, and Norway grew by close to two per cent annually, reflecting strong natural growth of the working-age population as well as a considerable rise in participation rates, of adult women in particular. In Europe, by contrast, the labour force grew by about ¼ per cent annually and participation rates barely changed.

Emigration is a key factor in any analysis of functioning of the Irish labour market. In view of the constraints on my time, suffice it here to recall that emigration traditionally acted as a safety valve in the labour market, mitigating the rise in unemployment in the 1980s (as it did in the 1960s). Without the pronounced fall in the participation rate (averaging −0.7 per cent annually) and the small decline in the labour force, Ireland would have seen a much larger rise in unemployment over the period 1983 to 1988.

I now turn to the broad patterns of adjustment that are suggested by the data and our empirical work. These may be thought of as systematic or partial interpretations of labour market institutions and developments in the 1980s, as they relate to macroeconomic performance. As can be imagined, there is no simple, readily available indicator capable of measuring the functioning of labour markets. Various summary indicators have been used to capture key characteristics of labour market performance. The most prominent of these measures is the NAIRU - the rate of unemployment needed to stabilize price inflation (NAIRU) or wage inflation (NAWRU). This is not the time to look at these summary indicators in detail, though it is important to recall that they have major limitations. Such measures can be taken as a proxy of structural unemployment, though they need to be used with care and in conjunction with additional indicators of performance and information about both institutions and policy.

Neverthless, the conclusions from the analysis done by the OECD and others on these indicators are of major importance. The significant deterioration in these measures observed from the early 1970s to the mid-1980s means that the level of unemployment 'needed' to contain inflation has risen over the last couple of decades. For the United States, Canada and Japan, the rise in structural unemployment has been small, while it has been large for the four major European countries as well as many of the smaller economies. This result can imply two things. In a world free of unexpected shocks, such increases may point to a fall in labour-market efficiency (increased malfunctioning), which may arise from a variety of sources, including increased trade-union militancy, increases in minimum wages or an easing of unemployment insurance provisions. When economies are hit by shocks, however, increases in the NAIRU and the rate of unemployment at the peak of the cycle may also reflect macroeconomic disequilibria and become a measure of the shock-absorbing power of labour markets (labour market flexibility). But it is clearly difficult to distinguish these two cases, without having supporting information on other aspects of the labour market.

As regards Ireland, emigration and, to some extent, lack of data render the efforts to calculate any of these summary indicators less than satisfactory, with results often contradictory or mixed at best. Given the Irish data on unemployment and inflation, which reveal a close negative association only since 1981, it is clear that labour market outcomes deteriorated significantly. For the same period, however, the OECD survey of Ireland noted that the sensitivity of wages to unemployment had increased, while their responsiveness to price increases appeared to have fallen. Hence, the degree of short-run real wage flexibility has increased. This is measured by the ratio of elasticity of nominal wages to the unemployment rate to the elasticity with respect to expected inflation; with 1.7, the measure is close to an average of 2.5 reported for an eleven-country sample of OECD economies. Unfortunately, the improvement in real wage flexibility is not confirmed when redoing the calculation while taking account of emigration. Rather the sensitivity of wages with respect to unemployment may have decreased during the 1980s, probably reflecting a widening tax wedge. Hence, the instability of the inflation-unemployment relationship is confirmed for Ireland, and controversial discussions will continue on the relevance of this indicator.

The variation among OECD countries in unemployment experience since the mid-1970s has given rise to a discussion about the impact of specific institutional arrangements in labour markets, in particular the structure of collective bargaining, on unemployment and inflation. The degree of centralisation of the wage bargaining structure and trade union power (e.g. union density, strike activity or the mark-up over non-union wages) are probably the broadest indicators of the institutional environment in which labour markets operate. In countries with highly centralised wage bargaining systems or high trade union memberships, the political representation of wage and salary earners is likely to be strong, and vice versa. This may effect the level of minimum wages, unemployment insurance benefits and outlays on active labour market programmes, which are subject to government legisltion and therefore represent rather direct indicators of labour-market policy broadly defined.

The OECD has analysed the relationship between collective bargaining structures, unemployment and inflation for the 1970s, a period of general inflation, and the 1980s, a period of widespread disinflation, for a sample of seventeen member countries. (Figure 3). The analysis considered both the average unemployment and inflation rates for the periods 1971-80 and 1981-86, and the changes in these measures from the beginning to the end of each period. The countries were combined into three broad groups of high, intermediate, and low centralisation of bargaining, which permits an analysis that is much less dependent on the exact ranking of individual countries.

The main results are:

1. On a country by country basis there appears to be no direct relationship between macroeconomic performance and bargaining structure in either the 1970s or 1980s.

2. However, countries with centralised bargaining had the lowest levels and smallest increases in unemployment rates during both the 1970s and 1980s. Countries with intermediate bargaining structures experienced the largest increases in unemployment.

3. On the other hand, the figure shows that the net change in inflation rates between 1971 and 1986 was virtually identical in the three groups of countries. However, countries with either centralised or decentralised bargaining arrangements had more volatile inflation rates, experiencing relatively large increases in the 1970s and large decreases in the 1980s.

FIGURE 3: *Relationship between collective bargaining structures, unemployment and inflation.*

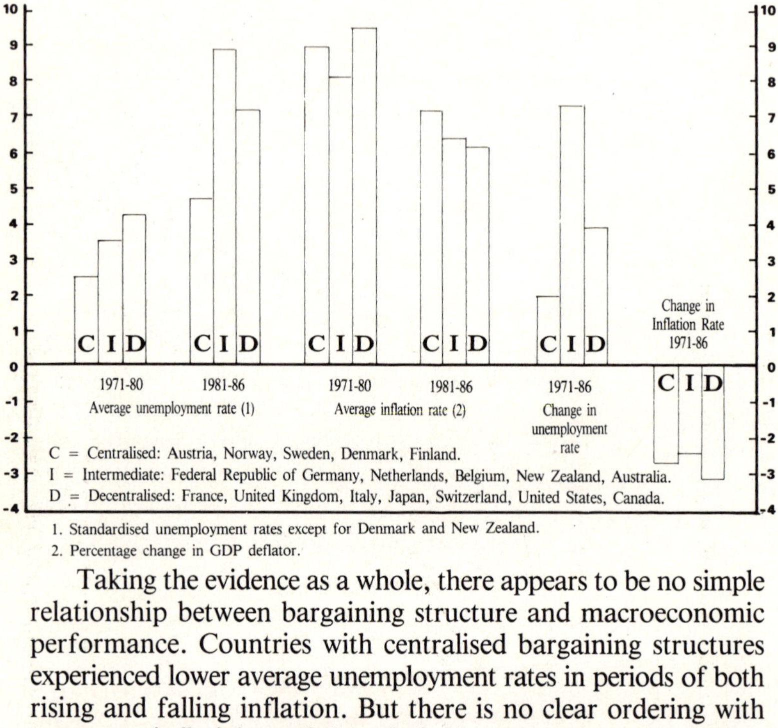


1. Standardised unemployment rates except for Denmark and New Zealand.
2. Percentage change in GDP deflator.

Taking the evidence as a whole, there appears to be no simple relationship between bargaining structure and macroeconomic performance. Countries with centralised bargaining structures experienced lower average unemployment rates in periods of both rising and falling inflation. But there is no clear ordering with respect to inflation, and the relative unemployment experience of countries with intermediate or decentralised structures reversed from the 1970s to the 1980s. Clearly other factors are important for unemployment and inflation performance.

This rather tentative assessment has been refined by netting out cyclical unemployment, which gives a proxy for the structural part of unemployment. Figure 4 shows that countries with small increases in non-cyclical unemployment are generally those with highly-centralised (Austria, Sweden, Denmark, and Finland) or highly-decentralised wage bargaining systems (Japan, Canada, United States, Switzerland). These are the two categories of countries that featured in the low-unemployment group of the overview table. The fact that labour-market outcomes can be favourable, nothwithstanding a set of sharply different institutional aspects, shows that interpretation of labour market indicators is complex. In contrast, judged by increases in both

FIGURE 4

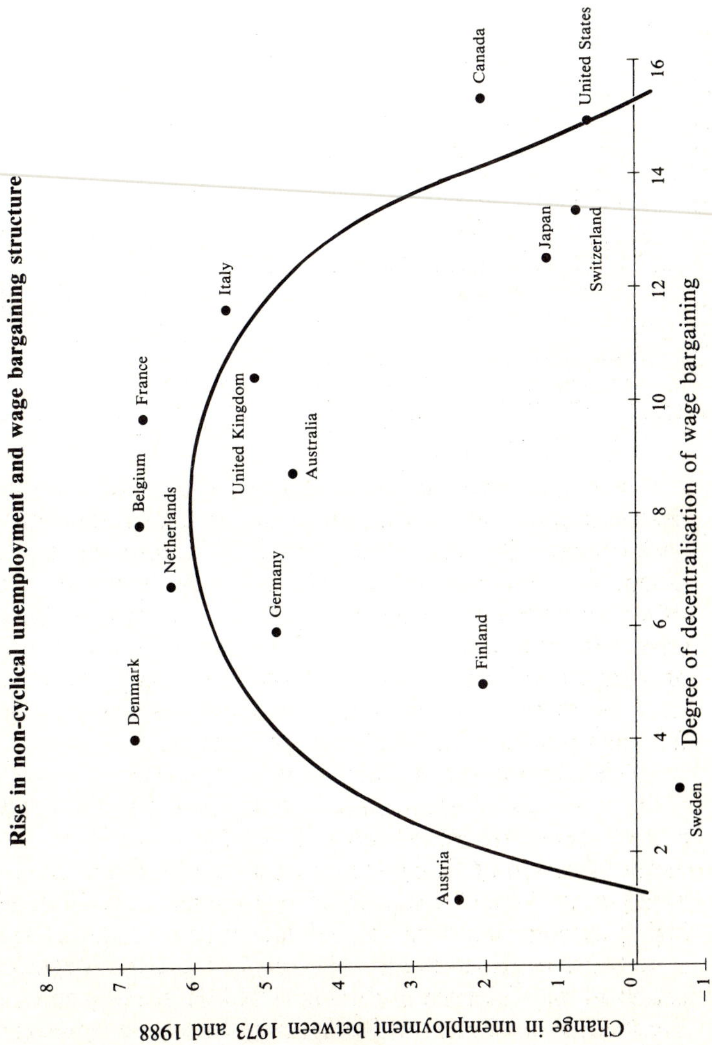
Rise in non-cyclical unemployment and wage bargaining structure
Change in unemployment between 1973 and 1988
Degree of decentralisation of wage bargaining
8
7
6
5
4
3
2
1
0
−1
2
4
6
8
10
12
14
16
Austria
Sweden
Denmark
Finland
Germany
Netherlands
Belgium
Australia
United Kingdom
France
Italy
Japan
Switzerland
Canada
United States

the NAIRU and non-cyclical unemployment, labour markets seem to function less well in countries with an intermediate position in terms of decentralisation or trade union membership (Germany, France, the United Kingdom, Italy, Belgium, the Netherlands, and Australia). These countries generally have moderately generous unemployment insurance provisions; small inter-industry wage differentials; high relative minimum wages (Belgium and the Netherlands); an above-average degree of lay-off and hiring restrictions (Germany, Italy and Belgium); and high government spending on active labour-market policies and subsidies.

According to this analysis, countries with highly centralised wage bargaining structures (Denmark, Finland, Sweden and, to a lesser extent Austria) are characterised by small wage differentials, generous unemployment insurance provisions and high outlays on active labour market programmes. In addition, all these countries have above-average subsidy/GDP ratios. The opposite configuration emerges for countries with highly decentralised systems (the United States, Japan, Canada, and Switzerland). These countries combine low trade-union membership with restrictive unemployment insurance provisions, low expenditure on active manpower policies, large inter-industry wage differentials and low subsidies. The ratio of non-wage labour costs and the severity of hiring and lay off restrictions appears unrelated to the degree of decentralisation of wage bargaining structures.

A further link between the performance of labour markets and their institutional structure can be established by plotting the measure of wage bargaining decentralisation against the measure of short-run real wage rigidity (Figure 5). As in the case of non-cyclical unemployment performance, a bell-shaped association is revealed. Countries appear to have similar degrees of short-run real wage rigidity in spite of sharply different degrees of centralisation of wage bargaining. This is borne out by a comparison betwen Australia, Finland and Sweden on the one hand and the United States, Japan, and Canada on the other. It also implies that a low measure of real wage rigidity is compatible with polar values for trade-union power, unemployment insurance provisions, wage differentials and outlays on active labour market programmes. The fact that labour market outcomes can be favourable, nothwithstanding

FIGURE 5

**Real wage rigidity(1) and the degree of corporatism(2)**

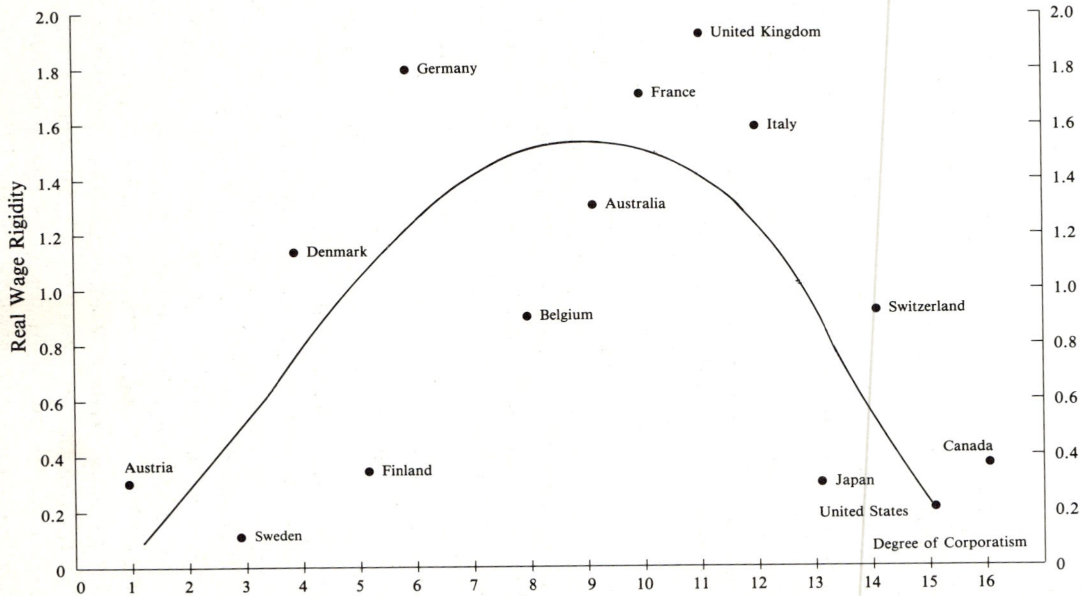


1. Real wage rigidity is measured by the short-run rigidity indicator reported in Table 2.6. It is calculated with a productivity impact for the following countries: United States, Japan, Germany, Belgium, Denmark, Sweden and Switzerland, which increases measured flexibility. For the United Kingdom, real wage rigidity is calculated from the specification excluding the hypothesis of hysteresis; hysteresis itself is an indication of low flexibility.

2. Countries are ranked from the most centralised (close to the origin) to the least centralised. The ranking is that used in Calmfors, Lars and Hohn Drifil (1988), 'Centralisation of wage bargaining and macroeconomic performance', *Economic Policy,* April. Also see OECD, *Economic Outlook 43,* June 1988.
*Source:* OECD Secretariat.

a set of sharply different institutional aspects, underlines the complexity of interpretation of labour market indicators. The previous finding is, however, confirmed; labour markets seem to function less well in countries with an intermediate position in terms of decentralisation or trade-union membership. Such countries where so-called fragmented bargaining prevails, are Germany, France, the United Kingdom, Italy, Belgium and the Netherlands. As can be seen, Ireland has not been included in the sample of the chart, given the inconclusive results which I reported. However, taking a range of 0.6 to 0.9 to real-wage rigidity for Ireland for whatever it's worth, Ireland would feature in an intermediate band together with Belgium and Switzerland, while the shift to decentralised wage-bargaining should in principle have moved her position in a south-easterly direction. Please note that the vertical axis is in terms of real wage rigidity, which is simply defined as the inverse of the real wage flexibility.

Besides short-run real wage flexibility, adaptability of employment interacting with the former, is another key element that contributes to labour market resilience. I will explain these notions, that are essential for the understanding of differences in how economies react to shocks. Employment adaptability is the speed with which employment adjusts to output changes. For a given degree of real wage flexibility, countries with highly adaptable employment would experience a quicker and greater rise in unemployment after a negative supply shock. This would in turn induce a stronger nominal wage moderation. Contrast this with a country where employment is more rigid; the nominal wage adjustment would be damped. In a sense, economies characterised by high real wage flexibility can afford some rigidity in employment adjustment: output can remain profitable (and thus viable) as flexible wages allow employment to be maintained. Japan and Austria would be the most striking exampes in this category. In the United States and Canada, where employment is highly adaptable, a pronounced rise in unemployment would exert a relatively strong moderating influence even though the elasticity of wages to unemployment is only average. The worst of both worlds is one where real wages are inflexible and employment not very adaptable: France, Belgium, the Netherlands and the United Kingdom appear to be in this category. If neither wages nor employment can adjust readily to changed conditions, the viability of enterprises risks being compromised, creating the danger of large-scale redundancies associated with bankruptcies.

I have emphasised that the information provided by aggregate, institutional and policy indicators needs to be complemented by a wide range of detailed indicators of labour-market structure (Table 2). These include: the share of long-duration unemployment in total unemployment as an indicator of human capital decay; the employment/population ratio as the broadest measure of underutilistion of labour; the youth unemployment rate as an indicator of a form of labour-market segmentation potentially costly to human capital development; the dispersion of regional unemployment rates as an indicator of regional imbalance, and perhaps of geographical mobility; and the vacancy rate as an indicator of labour market mismatch.

These indicators are valuable in providing evidence about the success and failure of specific labour market institutions and policies. Countries have been divided into three groups, of high, medium and low unemployment according to the standardised rates of unemployment in 1988. Given the relatively close correspondence between the measure of unemployment at cyclical peaks and NAIRU measures, the same sort of grouping would be arrived at using the latter.

Table 2 shows that countries may have a similar rate of overall unemployment, while the detailed indicators strongly diverge. Comparing Japan and Norway, countries with low unemployment, and France and Belgium, countries with high unemployment, illustrates this point. Japan has a large share of long-duration unemployment, which is small in Norway, while Norwegian youth unemployment is high relative to its ambitious labour market policies. Between France and Belgium, significant differences in the incidence of unemployment are noticeable, in particular regarding long-term unemployment, with three of four unemployed out of work for more than twelve months in Belgium, an indication of human capital decay substantially worse than in Ireland.

A review of the changes in the supplementary indicators that have occurred since the end-1970s reveals major shifts in the

Table 2: **Additional indicators of labour market performances in 1987 and 1988**

| Standardised rates of unemployment (1988) | Long-duration unemployment (b) | Youth unemployment rate (c) | Dispersion of regional unemployment (d) | Vacancy rate (e) | Employment/ population ratio (f) | Part-time employment (g) | Labour force growth (1973-88) (h) |
|---|---|---|---|---|---|---|---|
| 0.7 (a) | — | — | — | 0.43 | 71.1 | — | 0.2 |
| 1.0 (a) | — | — | — | — | — | — | 2.6 |
| 1.6 | 8.2 | 4.0 | 0.95 | 1.41 | 79.3 | 25.1 | 0.7 |
| 2.5 | 20.2 | 5.0 | 0.74 | 0.91 | 70.4 | 16.6 | 1.1 |
| 3.2 | 5.0 | 6.0 | 0.55 | 0.47 | 78.8 | 25.7 | 1.6 |
| 3.5 (a) | 10.8 | — | 0.44 | 0.89 | 64.3 | — | 0.4 |
| 4.5 | 19.0 | 9.0 | 2.24 | 0.65 | 72.4 | 8.1 | 0.8 |
| 5.4 | 8.1 | 10.3 | 2.12 | — | 69.5 | 17.3 | 2.1 |
| 5.6 | 56.6 | — | — | 0.19 | 65.2 | 6.0 | 1.8 |
| 6.0 (a) | — | — | — | 0.17 | 71.5 | — | 1.6 |
| 6.2 | 48.1 | 7.2 | 3.22 | 0.66 | 60.7 | 12.9 | 0.6 |
| 7.2 | 28.7 | 13.0 | 1.22 | 0.75 | 66.4 | 20.0 | 2.0 |
| 7.6 (a) | 45.8 | — | 1.19 | — | 54.3 | 5.8 | 1.3 |
| 7.7 | 9.4 | 11.5 | 3.58 | — | 68.1 | 15.4 | 2.5 |
| 8.3 | 45.2 | 14.5 | 3.03 | 0.87 | 58.7 | 21.6 | 0.8 |
| 8.6 (a) | 29.6 | — | 0.92 | 0.04 | 76.2 | 23.7 | 1.0 |
| 9.5 | 55.6 | — | 0.65 | 0.48 | 46.9 | 21.0 | 0.5 |
| 10.1 | 45.5 | 24.0 | 1.62 | 0.26 | 58.7 | 11.8 | 0.7 |
| 10.2 | 74.5 | — | 2.22 | 0.49 | 56.7 | 9.4 | 0.6 |
| 11.8 | 55.0 | 37.7 | 7.35 | — | 58.0 | 5.0 | 1.1 |
| 15.9(a) | — | — | — | — | 50.5 | — | 1.5 |
| 16.7(a) | 65.8 | — | 0.76 | — | 50.8 | 6.2 | 1.1 |
| 19.1 | 61.9 | 37.0 | 5.14 | 0.34 | 44.9 | — | 0.8 |

*Low-unemployment countries:* Switzerland, Iceland, Sweden, Japan, Norway, Austria, Finland.
*Intermediate group:* United States, Portugal, New Zealand, Germany, Australia, Greece, Canada, United Kingdom, Denmark, Netherlands.
*High-unemployment countries:* France, Belgium, Italy, Turkey, Ireland, Spain.

position of individual countries (Table 3). Using these satellite indicators, it is possible to identify three broad labour-market groups: one where structural labour-market conditions seem to have improved; another where such conditions seem to have deteriorated by a small amount, and a third where structural labour-market conditions seem to have worsened significantly.

Labour markets proved resilient in Portugal, Sweden, the United States and Finland. However Switzerland, Japan, Norway and Austria dropped out of the premier category, with the former two countries experiencing an increasing labour mismatch, and the latter two being marked by an increase in long-duration unemployment. Of those countries that saw a pronounced deterioration of labour market flexibility, the German case is very instructive, as four out of eight indicators point to a worsening on a number of fronts.

The detailed indicators of labour-market performance need to be seen in the light of the institutional and policy framework, which I have already sketched out (Table 4). To recall: the main constituents of this framework are the wage bargaining system, in particular, the role and power of trade unions and employers organisations; unemployment insurance and other social security provisions; wage differentials; lay-off and hiring restrictions, the minimum wage, non-wage labour costs, subsidies, income and payroll taxes, and public labour-market policies. Each of these features is amenable to policy action, though to differing degrees.

It has, I hope become evident by now that a diagnosis of malfunctioning of labour markets is not a straightforward matter at all. Nor are there broad policy lessons easily to be drawn from the smaller OECD countries' experience that are readily applicable to Ireland. Yet it is obvious that the sharp rise in unemployment, together with long-duration unemployment and the fall in the participation rate and labour supply growth, point to serious shortcomings of past policies and rigidities in the labour market. These prevent increases in labour demand through real wage adjustments in response to the increase in unemployment. The OECD has done a detailed analysis on the factors that lay behind Ireland's high increase in unemployment during the period of severe policy-induced demand restraint. This is published in

## Table 3: **Changes in Labour Market Peformance**

| Change in the standardised unemployment rate between 1979 and 1988 | Change in long-duration unemployment (1987 minus 1979) | Change in vacancy rate (1988 minus 1979) | Change in youth unemployment rate (1988 minus 1979) | Change in dispersion of regional unemployment (f) (1987 minus 1980-82) | Change in employment/ population ratio (1987 minus 1979) | Change in overall participation rate (1987 minus 1979) | Change in labour supply growth (g) (1979-88 minus 1973-79) |
|---|---|---|---|---|---|---|---|
| −2.6 | — | — | — | — | −0.6 | −3.0 | −1.94 |
| −0.5 | 1.4 | 0.25 | −1.0 | 0.01 | 0.4 | 2.5 | −0.28 |
| −0.4 | 3.9 | — | −1.0 | 0.20 | 2.9 | 3.1 | −1.07 |
| −0.1 (a) | −4.5 (b) | 0.15 (a) | −1.0 | −0.24 | 0.4 (b) | 1.5 | 0.08 |
| 0.4 | 3.7 | 0.22 | 1.6 | 0.12 | 0.1 | 0.7 | 0.01 |
| 0.4 | — | 0.14 | — | — | −2.4 | −1.3 | 1.15 |
| 0.3 | 7.9 | — | −1.5 | 0.40 | 2.9 | 4.3 | −1.50 |
| 1.2 | 1.2 | −0.05 | −0.06 | — | 4.5 | 5.5 | −0.53 |
| 1.5 (c) | 7.7 (d) | 0.24 (c) | 2.2 | 0.16 | −0.6 (d) | 3.0 | 0.60 |
| 1.8 | 2.2 | −0.05 | — | — | −3.3 | −2.7 | 0.07 |
| 1.7 | — | 0.12 | — | — | −2.1 | 6.9 | −0.99 |
| 2.0 | 16.5 | 0.36 | — | — | −2.7 | −0.7 | −0.73 |
| 2.3 | — | — | — | — | −8.8 | −8.8 | −0.28 |
| 2.4 | — | −0.04 | — | — | 1,8 | 3.0 | −0.28 |
| 3.0 | 28.2 | −0.47 | 3.5 | 1.98 | −3.9 | −0.7 | 1.00 |
| 3.3 | 20.4 | −0.04 | 3.2 | 0.72 | −2.6 | −0.3 | 0.14 |
| 4.1 | 28.5 (e) | −0.87 | — | — | −4.8 | 1.3 | 0.07 |
| 4.2 | 19.2 | — | 12.1 | 3.09 | −0.9 | 0.8 | 0.12 |
| 4.2 | 15.2 | −0.12 | 10.7 | 0.34 | −5.5 | −2.0 | −0.52 |
| 5.7 | — | — | — | — | −0.1 | 3.1 | 1.15 |
| 9.6 | 34.0 | — | — | — | −7.9 | 0.8 | −0.57 |
| 10.6 | 34.0 | — | 15.8 | — | −7.2 | 0.2 | 0.61 |

I. *Improvement or more change* (Labour market resilience) — Portugal, Sweden, United States, Finland.
II *Moderate Deterioration* — Japan, Switzerland, Canada, Norway, Australia, Austria, New Zealand, Belgium, Turkey, Denmark.
III *Pronounced deterioration* (labour market rigidity) — Germany, United Kingdom, Netherlands, Italy, France, Greece, Ireland, Spain.

## Table 4: **Changes in labour market practices**

| | United States | Japan | Germany | France | United Kingdom | Italy | Canada | Belgium | Finland | Ireland | Netherlands | New Zealand | Portugal | Spain | Sweden |
|---|---|---|---|---|---|---|---|---|---|---|---|---|---|---|---|
| 1. Short-run real wage rigidity[a] | Low | Low | Intermediate | High | High | Intermediate | Low | High | Low | Intermediate | High | High | Low | Intermediate | Low |
| 2. Intersectoral labour cost differentials[b] | Average | Average | Low | High | Low | High | Low | — | Low | Low | — | Low | Low | — | Low |
| 3. Change in (2) | Rising | Stable | Rising | Falling | Falling | Falling | Rising | — | Falling | Stable | — | — | — | — | Falling |
| 4. Inter-industry wage differentials[c] | High | High | Low | Low | Low | Average | High | Low | Low | Average | — | Low | — | — | Low |
| 5. Change in (4) | Rising | Rising | Rising | Falling | Falling | Falling | Stable | Falling | Rising | — | — | — | — | — | Falling |
| 6. Change in dispersion of intersectoral productivity differentials[d] | Falling | Stable | Rising | Rising | — | Falling | — | — | — | — | — | — | — | — | Rising |
| 7. Change in ratio of female to male wages[e] | — | Falling | Rising | Stable | Rising | Rising | — | Stable | Rising | Rising | Rising | Rising | Rising | — | Rising |
| 8. Change in ratio of female to male unemployment rate | Falling | Rising | Rising | Falling | Rising | Falling | Falling | Rising | Stable | Stable | Rising | Stable | Stable | Rising | Falling |
| 9. Change in ratio of youth to adult wages | Falling | Stable | — | Stable | Rising | — | Falling | — | Stable | — | — | — | Stable | — | Rising |
| 10. Change in ratio of youth to adult unemployment rates | Falling | Falling | Rising | Rising | Rising | — | Falling | — | Rising | — | — | — | Stable | Falling | Rising |
| 11. Minimum wages[f] | Low falling | Not relevant | No legal minimum | High stable | Not relevant | No legal minimum | Low falling | Lower rate for youth | — | Not relevant | High falling | Not relevant | Low stable | Average falling | No legal minimum |
| 12. Unemployment replacement rates[g] | Low | Low | High | High | Low | Average | Average | High | High | High | — | Average | Low | Low | High |
| 13. Change in part-time employment relative to full-time employment | Small increase | Small increase | Strong rise | Strong rise | Small absolute | Average rising | Small rise | Strong rise | — | — | Strong rise | Average rise | — | — | Strong rise |
| 14. Change in annual hours worked per employed person | Small fall | Small rise | Average fall | Strong decline | Strong decline | Small decline | Average fall | — | Average fall | — | Average fall | Average fall | — | — | Average fall |
| 15. Earnings exempt from employers' social security contributions | Zero | Intermediate | Intermediate | Zero | High | High | Low | — | — | — | — | — | — | — | — |
| 16. Rise in unemployment relative to high capacity use (shift in 'Okun curve') | Small | Small | Moderate | Strong | Strong | Strong | Moderate | Strong | Small | Strong | Strong | Small | Small | Strong | Small |

*a)* Short-run price coefficients divided by cyclical coefficient (money wage equations for private non-farm business sector).
*b)* Coefficient of variation of sectoral labour cost differentials (compensation per employed person).
*c)* Coefficient of variation of inter-industry hourly wage differentials (compensation per employed person).
*d)* Coefficient or variation of sectoral output per employed person.
*e)* Hourly adult wages.
*f)* Relative to the wage of average productive workers.
*g)* Unemployed benefits per unemployed person as a percentage of net income of average production worker.
*Sources: F. Klau and A. Mittelstadt (1986); J. Chan-Lee, D. Coe and M. Prywes (1987); and subsequent updating.*

the OECD Economic Surveys. The findings point to the following major impediments to better functioning labour markets (Figure 6)

FIGURE 6: **The Irish tax wedge**

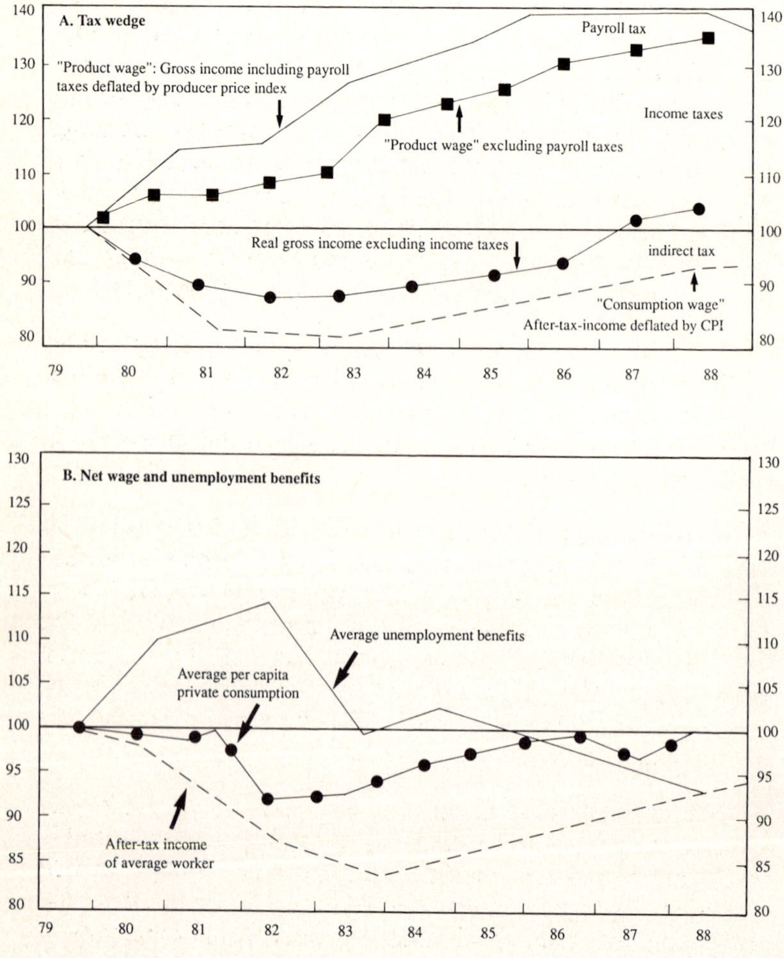


1. Includes net social security contributions.
2. Includes terms of trade effects.

**Source: OECD; for details see technical notes.**

1. Continued increase in real labour costs despite the decline in real take-home pay per employee. Because of increasing direct and indirect taxes, real after-tax wages of the average employee fell by 15 per cent between 1979 and 1983, while real labour costs to firms rose by 12 per cent. This 'tax wedge' has widened since 1983 by another eight percentage points.

2. A high 'income replacement ratio' measured as unemployment compensation as a percentage of take-home pay. High replacement ratios increase the average duration of unemployment by prolonging job search. When the utility derived from leisure is included, a 'welfare trap' may result for individuals with low earnings potential, making unemployment more attractive than employment. The replacement ratio increased significantly between 1979 and 1982 but has since declined substantially, mainly due to a continuous reduction in average real unemployment benefits, by a total of 15 per cent.

3. Government regulations to protect employees rights and conditions of employment may have had an adverse effect on hiring, shifting the demand for labour to fixed-term contracts of less than a year, to which this legislation is not applicable.

4. Industrial policy has distorted relative factor prices in favour of capital and against labour despite increasing excess labour supply. In fact, the annual average labour productivity growth of 0.9 per cent registered over the period 1979 to 1987 can more than fully be accounted for by the acceleration in capital-labour substitution. However the policy has been reviewed recently and changes have been initiated.

Before elaborating on each of these points, I will make one general observation. Policies conducive to sustainable employment growth should have priority. Public deficit reduction, through its effect of lowering real interest rates, and tax reform both tend to stimulate investment and employment growth. Both efficiency considerations and the current fiscal position preclude the use of public expenditure for direct employment creation. The large increase in employment required to absorb the present high unemployment and the rapid natural increase in the labour force must therefore come from private sector initiative.

Regarding tax reform, existing marginal tax rates on personal income are among the highest in the OECD area, although social security charges are relatively low. High marginal tax rates are likely to stifle effort and initiative, and to induce enterprising and skilled members of the labour force to leave the country. At the same time, average effective tax rates are rather low, reflecting large exemptions from the tax base and/or tax concessions. Broadening the tax base thus offers considerable scope to lower marginal tax rates, which should generate beneficial supply-side effects. Such a policy need not be to the detriment of prevailing equity objectives, since many of the existing tax exemptions and concessions benefit high income earners disproportionately. A significant start has been made on broadening the tax base and reducing the marginal tax rates in recent budgets.

As to labour markets, it is important to permit these to function properly, with real wages developing at the economy-wide level in a way that reflects excess supply in the labour market, and with relative wage developments reflecting relative skill scarcities. Insistence on historical wage differentials without regard for relative skill scarcities is inconsistent with this objective and should therefore be resisted. The present large excess supply of labour clearly makes wage restraint desirable, which is also consistent with the need to maintain international competitiveness.

As regards industrial policy, Ireland over the last twenty years has succeeded in attracting highly efficient export-producing international companies by granting generous investment subsidies and tax concessions. The urgent need for fiscal consolidation makes it difficult to pursue these policies on the previous scale. In addition there are legitimate doubts whether this policy approach to industrial development is efficient. The recent reduction in the scale of investment subsidies, and a reorientation of aid to industry towards marketing and technology transfer, are steps in the right direction.

In summing up and recalling the different policy paradigms that I sketched out in the introduction (Figure 1, bottom panel, left), it might be asked whether Ireland has not now reached a stage of development at which heavy government involvement in decisions on where to invest and which activities to support, risks becoming counter-productive. Practical experience and new insights from public choice theory have convinced policy makers in many OECD countries that these decisions should be left as far as possible to the market. The government's role would be mainly to minimise distortions to market decisions by establishing a tax system which is as neutral as possible with respect to resource allocation. Strict adoption of this principle, or even more modestly a move to a level of intervention typical of OECD countries generally, would require further adjustments in current Irish industrial policy, while cautious macroeconomic policies need to be maintained.

COLM McCARTHY

# Outline for the 1990s - A Decade of Fiscal Restraint?

I WOULD like to begin my presentation by reviewing performance in the macro economy over the last few years. We are all aware that things have changed somewhat since around 1985/86 when the outlook seemed rather gloomy. However, matters have now improved, and I would like to run through what I think has been happening over that period. One of the most striking indicators of performance is the level of EBR (Exchequer Borrowing Requirement) as a percentage of GNP. In 1986 it was about 13% of GNP, and latest estimates for 1989 put it at about 3%, which means that ten percentage points will have been cut out of central government borrowing in three years and I can't recall any situation, in this part of the world, where a country has cut its government borrowing quite as quickly as that. However, I think it is also worth reviewing what happened in the years before that dramatic improvement in the public finances took place.

Around 1980/81 there was pretty general agreement here that there was something wrong with the public finances and that we ought to do something about the situation. There was a series of elections around that period and this issue dominated them. Somehow or other we didn't manage to do much about it in the subsequent five years or so. There were two reasons for this. One was that the economy was very depressed over this period and although the international economy did recover, it wasn't so strong either in the early part of the decade. Secondly tax revenues in Ireland right through the years up to 1986 and into 1987 were very sluggish and that, of course, made any recovery in the fiscal position difficult. On top of that, public expenditure in real terms actually rose over that period and there were various political difficulties in tackling it. So I think the fact that there was no great progress made on the public finance problem in the early 1980s can really be put down to those two factors. There were, however, some economic policy achievements over this period. Inflation was nearly 20% in 1981 and it was cut very dramatically through adherence to the fixed exchange rate EMS discipline. The external payments deficit, which had been alarmingly high in the early 1980s was also brought under control.

In effect it was the budget of 1987 that commenced the process of containment of public expenditure. On top of that, tax revenues have ever since continuously outstripped government forecasts. All of this, of course, in contrast with the early 1980s was achieved against a very favourable international climate. The recent growth in tax revenue has largely been fuelled by the very strong domestic economic recovery of the last few years. This recovery has been due, I think, to a range of factors some of which were certainly not the result of government action. Two direct effects of policy, however, were a lower level of public spending than would have otherwise arisen, and a restoration of financial market confidence which helped to bring down interest rates. I think it is reasonable to credit the huge turn around in government finances over these last few years to roughly equal measurements of good management and good luck! The revenue buoyancy, as already stated, was way ahead of what the government anticipated.

GNP growth over this period has really been very uneven. Real GNP actually fell in 1985 and 1986, and there has really only been any sustained growth in the last few years. In 1989 most forecasters expect a 5% growth in real GNP, with every expectation of something similar in 1990. It seems to me that we are now in a rather curious situation. We had an election in June 1989 which was fought around a very narrow range of issues in relation to whether you wanted to re-elect the government, with some side-shows about health cuts (both real and imagined). What has actually happened is that the government in 1987 did two things; first of all it said that the public finance situation had to be corrected, and it established that as its main policy plank, and secondly it concluded an important industrial relations and pay deal with the trade unions. The economic policy agenda that the government set itself in 1987 has actually largely been completed. With a 3% exchequer borrowing requirement the ratio of debt to GNP is actually falling; it may still be far too high - but it's falling. Unless we are very unlucky the principal item on the 1987 policy agenda is being dealt with. I think that means therefore that on that issue we now need to have some new targets and some new intentions about the public finances. The government now needs to think about a new medium term macroeconomic strategy.

I would like to set out some issues which I feel need to be addressed in that context; and there are five that I would like to mention in particular. The first is public expenditure. We have been through three years now where there has been an attempt to exercise greater control over public spending. The question now arises as to whether it is necessary for government to continue with tight spending controls. The second issue is pay. The pay deal is finished next year and the question now is, should there be another one at all or should we go for decentralised bargaining again? Furthermore if there is another pay deal what should it involve? The third issue for consideration is taxation. I think that there is a lack of clarity about government intentions in this area. We don't appear to have made up our minds yet about what the main parameters of tax reform are going to be. Everybody is in favour of tax reform so long as it means that other people should pay more tax than I should. However, at the practical level we really don't have an agenda. The fourth issue is borrowing targets. We have now already achieved the borrowing target which the government said would be achieved by 1993, so it seems to me that we now need to have something else in its place. The fifth and final macro policy question is exchange rate policy.

On the question of whether we need to continue to contain public spending, I think it is unambiguous that we do. There is a widespread perception that we have actually cut public expenditure in Ireland over the past few years. In fact, under most headings that is not true at all. All that has happened is that the very rapid real increases in public expenditure which characterised the late '70s and early '80s have been brought under control. It is true that there have been actual falls in spending under some of the capital programme headings. On the current side, however, under most headings, (for example public service pay) there hasn't actually been a fall in real terms in public expenditure. It seems to me that we have to continue with the attempt to contain the growth in public spending. First of all, that will facilitate the attainment of any given borrowing target. It will also, of course, free resources for those taxation reforms that people want. There is a further aspect to this. The fact that government borrowing may soon be close to zero, and I think that is quite likely, does not necessarily mean that expenditure and revenue are balanced at the right level. There is a difference between drawing nil - nil in a football match and drawing 7 - 7. The fact that we have a level of expenditure and revenue that are in better balance doesn't mean that expenditure and revenue might not be too high. Most people 'half' agree with this. They all think government revenue is too high, in other words that taxes are too high. However people are slower to accept that the same consideration applies to the expenditure side. It seems to me that there is still a case for careful expenditure control at any level of overall borrowing, and indeed there remain many areas of public spending which at least some people would question in terms of value for money. There is also the question of political climate. Any perception that government resolve had weakened in the area of public expenditure containment could easily reactivate the public spending carnival which was at the root of the Irish economic debacle of the 1980s in the first instance.

On the question of pay, a new pay deal with the trade unions will presumably be negotiated during 1990. In principle, the government has the option of saying 'lets have a completely decentralised free collective bargaining situation'. In other words the government's attention would be restricted to public service pay, which is what happened some years back. At the moment, however, it looks as if the government will at least attempt to negotiate a new national agreement with the unions, employers, and farmers during 1990.

One ingredient in any such process will be that the inflation rate, having previously bottomed out around 2 - 2.5%, has begun to rise a little recently as indeed it has in some other countries. The last figure available was around 4.5%. It seems to me that a continuation of inflation at that level would doubtless see the unions seeking a pay increase of 6% or more. There are reasons to believe, however that the recent rise in inflation will prove temporary. Inflation has peaked in the continental European countries with which the Irish currency is now linked and it also appears to have finally peaked in the United Kingdom. The government may also feel that indirect tax reductions will be necessary from 1990 onwards in the context of EEC plans for fiscal harmonization, and this will moderate inflation further.

On the tax side, government decisions about direct taxes on income will inevitably impact on pay negotiations. The most obvious immediate option would be to cut the 32% standard income tax rate to 30%. We have heard a number of politicians recently talk about the medium term objective of getting the standard rate of income tax down to 25% over 3 - 5 years. It seems to me that there will certainly be a temptation to cut the 32% rate to 30%. If that were done in the 1990 budget there would of course be a substantial impact on post-tax pay, and for many workers take-home pay would be boosted by as much as 3%. The effect of any cut in income tax is greater, the higher your income, of course, since income tax is a progressive tax and this is a feature of the various reductions in income tax that we have seen (improvements in allowances etc.) in recent years. If you cut a progressive tax it always benefits the better off more then the worse off. Indeed, if you are really badly off you don't pay any tax to begin with. So, any attempt to use the improved public finance position we now have to reduce income tax is inevitably going to benefit better off people more than those at the very bottom of the income distribution. If, for example, it were desired to give a special boost to those on lower incomes, the way to do it is actually to cut employees social insurance contributions, since this tax is regressive. There are no allowances and there is an upper limit beyond which no tax is payable. It has often puzled me that trade unions in Ireland continually talk about the PAYE worker when, if the concern is really about lower income people in employment, employees PRSI is the tax that should really be targeted.

On the question of borrowing targets I mentioned at the outset that Exchequer borrowing will probably only be about 3% of GNP in 1989. Not so long ago this figure was the Government's target figure for 1993. It is now appropriate that a fresh look should be taken at the shape of fiscal policy over the next few budgets. I think there's a case for trying to move reasonably soon into a situation of small exchequer surplus. The case for doing so contains a number of elements. The first is the need to manage any tendency towards a slippage into external payments deficit. If private consumption and investment demand continue to surge ahead in 1990 as they have been doing throughout 1989, I think a slippage into external payments deficit becomes a serious possibility. A tightening of fiscal policy would then be required and that most probably means aiming for a surplus by 1991. Secondly, while we've managed to get the borrowing figures looking a bit healthier, the outstanding level of debt will still be over 100% of GNP even by budget time in 1992, and that's an uncomfortably high level of national debt to live with in the long term. Unless this can be reduced it leaves the economy cruelly exposed to high interest rates or to an appreciation of those currencies in which the external portion of the debt is denominated. I don't think we really want to run a level of national indebtedness as high as that forever. Finally there is a pure 'value for money' argument. Every hundred pounds by which the debt can be reduced will take about £9 or £10 off next year's tax bill because such are the levels of interest rates right now. Indeed interest rates are way above inflation rates and so anybody who's in debt at the moment is paying a very high real rate of interest. The point is that now is a particularly attractive time to be repaying debt if you can afford to do it.

The final pillar of macro policy is exchange rate policy. Adherence to the European Monetary System has been a central element in economic policy here since 1979. More importantly, the rate has been effectively fixed against the Deutsch Mark for roughly three years now. The government clearly intends to operate a fixed exchange rate against the German currency at the present level of around 2.65 or 2.66 DM. If there were to be another EMS realignment it seems to me that there would be little interest in changing that rate. The commitment of the Government was underlined by its decision to issue a dual currency bond earlier this year, with redemption in dividends in Irish or German currency at the option of the holder. Irish interest rates now track German rates more closely than they do UK rates, and the strong link between the Irish currency and the DM has made it possible for Irish-based lending rates to dip as much as 4% below UK rates during most of 1989. A further practical consideration is that German fund managers have now become major players in the Irish financial markets. It's estimated that German holders now account for about a quarter of all Irish pound denominated government securities in issue. The retention of German interest in the Irish Gilt market provides a further incentive for Government to stick to the current policy of a fixed exchange rate against the German unit.

So the main suggestions I'm making about macro policy are: (1) to stick to the fixed exchange rate with the DM in the event that there is a realignment over the next twelve/eighteen months. It seems to me that the fixed rate we've had with the DM for the last few years has worked fine and I don't think we should change it. (2) I mentioned that the exchequer borrowing requirement this year will be about 3% of GNP. The economy is growing quite quickly and so even if we did nothing it would fall next year. If we did nothing the year after we would probably be in surplus in 1991 without extra expenditure cuts or anything of that nature. There is genuine revenue buoyancy in the system now, so it seems to me that it makes sense to aim for an exchequer surplus from 1991 onwards. More generally I think the government should now deliberate a bit as to what its medium term fiscal policy targets are, given that its original targets have been achieved. (3) On the third issue of tax concessions, I would like to suggest that the Irish economy could now become vulnerable to a loss of competitiveness through the appreciation of the exchange rate. We've already seen this in relation to Sterling and there is not very much we can do about it. However if we also experience big pay demands and pay concessions on top of such a currency appreciation, that could erode at least some of the significant improvements in competitiveness that we've achieved over the last few years. To the extent therefore, that the Government has money to give away in the 1990 budget, I believe that tax concessions should be structured in such a way as to help to keep pay costs under control.

To me that means that perhaps they should be biased a bit towards indirect tax cuts, some of which will have to come anyway in the long term. I would argue that income tax cuts should be left on the agenda for the 1991 budget. I also made the point, and would like to emphasise it once again, that there is a choice between whether you cut income tax or PRSI - a choice that does affect the distributional impact of any tax concessions that are made. (4) Finally, on the question of expenditure control, I really don't think that there's any responsible argument for not continuing with the containment of public spending that we've seen over the last few years. Obviously there may be areas, from time to time, that might be exempted from that, for social policy or for other reasons, but I certainly don't believe that we should allow ourselves to become involved in some universal relaxation of expenditure control.

I would like now to look to the future a little, and consider the shape of the public finance question in the years ahead. I mentioned that the borrowing requirement would be about 3% of GNP in 1989. Possibly 1.5% in 1990, and then into surplus by 1992. Assuming a growth rate of 4% or 5% in the economy over the next few years, we are going to witness a gradual fall in the Debt/GNP ratio. It's still very high right now but in three to four years time it will fall below 100% of GNP. There is nothing magical about that number, but the point I'm making is that if we go along the route I've outlined, which I don't think would represent in any way a terribly tight fiscal policy, then I think it's possible that in four or five years time the overall debt situation in central government would begin to look a lot less intimidating than it does now. There's also of course the question of external payments, and we've seen in the UK and to some extent in Denmark, that during a period of fiscal adjustment, government tightens and tightens and eventually runs into surplus. However, private expenditure may go through the roof and so you wind up with an external payments deficit, which of course is what has happened in the UK. I would suggest then that, especially under a fixed rate, government must stand ready to tighten fiscal policy further to defend the exchange rate if private expenditure looks like it's too buoyant. I think it would be too early to say that such a phenomenon is happening here just yet but we can't rule it out over the next few years, and it may be that government will have to run a fiscal policy that is a little tighter than they really wanted because of external payments pressures.

I would like to say just a few words about our policy objectives in terms of the balance of payments. The balance of payments deficit represents the excess of investment over saving, and there appears to be a pervasive belief in this country that investment is too low at any level of saving. In parallel with this we find an entirely contradictory concern about payments deficits. It makes sense to invest heavily and run the associated payments deficits if returns on capital are high enough. If they're not, the policy will progressively erode real income. It's clear to me that returns on investment are now perceived to be much better than they were a few years ago, and investment is already rising very sharply in response. However that rise in investment should be accompanied by an eventual fall in the marginal efficiency of capital.The optimum level of investment is finite but to listen to some people in this country you would imagine that it wasn't.

In the 1990 budget the overall fiscal stance will be overshadowed in the minds of many by the taxation measures taken, but it seems to me that that budget is the first step in enunciating the Government's new medium term economic macro strategy, and I think therefore that the issue should dominate their concern. The kind of strategy I've outlined is particularly vulnerable to what might be termed 'generalised impatience' with the pace of progress. It's already clear that unemployment has fallen to a great extent because of emigration; there is job creation but it's slow. Invariably people are always disappointed because their incomes are not as high as they would like them to be and we're already seeing some evidence, I think of this 'generalised impatience' with the pace of economic recovery. Already there are calls for accelerated Government action on various fronts, usually with some socially disadvantaged group at the front of the platform, and the usual collection of producer lobbies waiting in the wings. It seems to me that it took the best part of a decade to create the economic mess from which the country has now spent just three years extricating itself, and in any realistic calculation there's at least another four or five years to go before a major impact becomes visible in areas like unemployment, emigration and the alleviation of the low income problem. In my view a patient perseverance with the approach of the last few years is now the only formula with a realistic chance of success.

MARC BATTAILLE

# Prosperity in Europe — The Roles of Industry and Government

I WOULD like to begin by asking a question: 'Who are the most important, convinced Europeans today within the EC? I will tell you: the Japanese. The Japanese understand very well how the EC operates. They understand the economic and political system and they know how to work it. When,for example, Spain and Portugal joined the EC on the 1 January 1986, Japan had already made massive investments in Spain and suddenly on that glorious day became an 'ex officio' member of the EC. I would just like to warn you that we have the Horse of Troy here in Europe. When we talk about prosperity, we mean bringing prosperity to this country in the 1990s and of course, by implication, into a larger European Community. Before we can talk prosperity, however, we have to solve a number of problems that we all face.

Europe is now home to a great number of political and economic refugees, not only from the developing countries, but also and perhaps more significantly we now have the new immigrants from the economies of Eastern Europe. This issue alone raises very serious questions about how all of these people are going to adapt to, or integrate within, their western European host countries. There is also a tremendous drug problem in Europe which we cannot afford to ignore. There will need to be much greater co-operation between the public and private sectors in trying to find an answer to this problem. We have enormous problems with crime in Europe. Indeed so sophisticated is this crime nowadays, and such is the vast amount of money which has been accumulated, that even very large funds can move through the international banking system without interference. There really are no national solutions to these issues. These are problems which require a common European approach. So before attempting to build greater prosperity, we will need to develop much more co-operation amongst each other. I believe that in the 1990s as we attempt to solve all this, we will find that nobody can do it on their own. The private sector cannot do it on its own. The public sector cannot do it on its own. We must therefore have a common effort and there are indeed models which we might consider.

The cases of Sweden and Finland illustrate this point. I am always impressed that wherever I travel these countries have very experienced commercial counsellors in their embassies. Where do these people come from? They come from the private sector. These two countries have a system whereby somebody from the private sector can go for three years to become a Diplomat, and then return to his private business. I find this very stimulating because it has helped to create a unique network in the Diplomatic Service of Sweden and Finland. As a result business people come to know each other and they know the senior civil servants. There is therefore a kind of camaraderie which operates for the benefit of the country; for Sweden and for Finland. As an illustration of this, I have been very struck by the fact that in order to get a good analysis of the situation in Tokyo, I can go to the Swedish Embassy, because a member of the Embassy staff there (a former and future business man) who was on loan for three years, has recently produced a fantastic paper giving a succinct overview of the commercial and economic situation in Japan.

There are of course other forms of collaboration. The Japanese achieve it with MITI. You know of course that the overall Ministry is now so powerful in Japan that people are lured to it after a successful career in private business and vice versa.

So there are numerous models of co-operation and we must never forget that all the challenges I referred to earlier can only be met through a very close co-operation. We have talent on both sides and we have experience on both sides. The public and private sectors should not look at each other in a doubtful or sceptical way. We must address these issues jointly. We are moving towards the year 2000, and although the '1990s' is a very nice title nevertheless 2000 is the day after tomorrow. It is only a decade away. So we must engage in joint dialogue; we must set up structures where you can say "we need to debate this or that problem". Earlier today, Dr Fest of the OECD gave us an enlightening presentation on aspects of the labour market. Nowadays many countries talk about early retirement. We have it in Belgium: people retire at 58, sometimes 56. I have heard that in France there is a strike going on at the moment because people want the option to retire at 54. How then are we going to cope with the needs of an active retired population in the years ahead? The total population is growing older at a staggering rate. So, as we say 'Yes — we are going to have early retirement', we must remember that we still need all the labour expertise we can get. As a businessman I have only one question: who is going to pay for all of this? Who is going to pay, particularly when we see that in many countries the social security resources are not at all that strong? I would suggest also that we are facing the future with very old and out-dated laws and regulations. I believe now is the time to use a little imagination and ask our legislators, 'is it not now appropriate in this fantastic era of information and technology, to consider making laws (which might be called "Sunset Laws") that are only valid for three to five years, and which must then be reviewed?'

There is now a fantastic dynamic within Europe. There is a kind of Euro-optimism, as if Europe is going to provide the solution to everything. My view is that we are still all different and that a common market does not necessarily mean a uniform market. We need these differences, for it is upon them that we are going to build. For the moment there is the exercise in harmonisation of laws — in harmonising the way that there can be movement across this large market of goods and services, of finances and people. Earlier today when I heard about services and services industry, it reminded me that the major part of EC spending on the consultancy business is taken by the UK. For you in Ireland now is the time to take part of that market. You have excellent consultancy services and there is no reason why the bulk of the money should go in the direction of Britain. If you are part of a team, then the resources should be passed around the team members. There should be equal access for all. We need therefore to consider the purpose and distribution of programme funding; it should never just be a case of 'let's grab the money'.

**International environment**

I would like to start with a comparison of working hours. Our friends in Japan work a total of 2166 hours per year while in the USA the figure is 1912. Total working hours in France are 1763 and in Germany 1760. We will need therefore to improve our performance more than just a little in order to stay competitive internationally. Furthermore, when I look through the total paid holidays (i.e. annual leave and public holidays), I find it is exactly the reverse. Whereas the Japanese have only 16 days paid holidays, workers in the USA have 27. But the champions in this regard are Belgium, France and the Netherlands with 42 days each. If we look at the area of third level education we find 110 vacation days in France, Belgium, and the Netherlands; 93 in the USA but only 63 in Japan. I must therefore, as a practical businessman, raise the issue of our productivity. It's easy to talk about the need for working smarter and working harder, but it's certainly not easy to make it happen. It involves a complete change of mentality which must take place if Europe is to avoid becoming complacent. We are now experiencing the globalisation of business, and it is not alone Japan that we should be concerned with. Korea, Taiwan and Singapore, for example, are all making rapid industrial progress, with consequent inroads into the European market-place.

I should also like to mention that while we in Europe offer generous support to the Newly Industrialised Countries, we find that significantly less is forthcoming from the US. I think it is about time that we approached the US with a view to working out some form of partnership arrangement in this regard.

One of the biggest problems that I see is the ageing pyramid, and the types of social and industrial circumstances which this will give rise to in the future. We have, for example, the rich old millions of the Triad countries (i.e North America, Japan and Europe). Then there are the poor young billions of the non-Triad countries; that is the poor billions of people who are outside the industrialised world. It is noteworthy that back in 1900 the the ten largest cities in the world were all in the Triad sector. However current projections reveal that in the year 2000 (which is only ten years from now), only two of the ten largest cities will be Triad ones, i.e. Tokyo (24m) and New York (22.8m). The other eight cities will be from the non-Triad sector and will include for example, Mexico city (31m) and Sao Paulo (25.8m), with all the consequent problems of pollution and overcrowding created by cities of this magnitude. Of even greater concern is the future of Africa. I often feel that we have abandoned the continent altogether. Is it going to be the swamp or the pit? Will the population suffer further decline in worsening malnutrition people going to die with the widespread incidence in Africa of the AIDS disease? I had occasion recently to sit in on a private meeting of Ministers of Foreign Affairs from Africa who were talking about the AIDS disease. One Minister said 'For us it is very simple; we went to the people and said "we don't have the money to help you; we don't have money for research or hospitals, so we advise you to go calmly home, not to the hospitals because we don't have the places, and to die calmly at home". People are slow to realise that in Zaire, Angola, Botswana, and other countries many tens of thousands of people have the disease; but these countries don't want to talk about it. So these are some issues we must think about before we talk prosperity.

There are always going to be winners and losers — nations and companies, because an ideal situation doesn't exist. We are entering a new technology wave where developments in micro-electronics and bio-technology will offer us the prospect of new solutions. We already have what I would call 'world class companies' which are established on a global basis. I would immediately cite Honda as a case in point. Honda have carefully developed a global influence. This is the big difference between the US Corporate sector, with its emphasis on the 'quarterly review' and its continual concern to have a good show at the stock exchange, (even if a couple of days later the picture has changed again), and at the other extreme the Japanese with their emphasis on careful planning. The Japanese accept (and indeed plan for) the fact that it might take them twenty-five years to reach their goal. You heard in the Philips presentation that they have already reached their goals in the photographic, watch and automobile industries and that they are well on their way to reaching it in the pharmaceutical industry. For the Japanese it's like planting a tree; it may take twenty-five years, but still they will methodically develop the competitive edge needed to conquer the world in any chosen economic sector. This therefore is the attitude we must adopt. This is how we must change, and in fact one of the major benefits of the EC is that it enables us to pool our resources together. There are already many programmes where we co-operate. However we need to develop further this cross-European co-operation, and in particular to develop closer ties between the universities and industry.

**Portrait of the winning nation**

I would like to show you the portrait of a winning nation, particularly as it might relate to Ireland in the 1990s. For me the portrait of a winning nation is one with a very high level of education. Today many people are asking, 'What is going to be the secret for the 1990s' — for taking on the challenges that we see around us?. I have only three answers — Education, Education, Education. If you look at employment trends on the continent you will find that more and more of the jobs which ten years ago required a high school diploma, are now being filled by university graduates. Increasingly this will mean that the real winners will be those people who can offer something more than all the others. This may mean two university degrees, possibly three university degrees. Competition for employment is going to become increasingly difficult, because there has emerged in recent years a 'de facto' erosion of the value of the university degree, due largely to the democratisation of the educational process. My own observations in Belgian universities lead me to believe that the students regard it as a necessary evil to go to university. Nowadays they want to finish as quickly as possble, and regard their degree purely as an entry to the jobs market, and to the service industries in particular. We are moving towards a tremendous explosion in the service industry, and it's in this area that we will need all the brains, all the talent and every possible effort in order to help us win.

The winning nation is also a nation which can mobilise capital very quickly, because in business today there are many occasions when you have to act very quickly, and have immediate access to capital. In Europe today we are dealing with a 'dual logic' economy. It is a dual logic economy between Italy on the one hand, (where they keep three or four sets of books!) and on the other, those countries where the application of the taxation laws is rigid in the extreme. Indeed I would suggest that the former type of dynamic is not necessarily a bad thing as long as the money stays in the country. This of course is the richness of Taiwan, Singapore and Hong Kong, where people work day and night, and there is a small level of official intervention. I am not, however advocating tax irregularity. I'm saying such things exist in European countries. Italy is a country doing very well economically, but I would argue that it is doing so on the basis of a 'dual logic' economy. Furthermore, we will have to accept that in the nation of European countries we cannot expect to abolish this immediately. It is not going to change overnight on the 1 January 1993. It's going to take a long time; a common market does not mean a uniform market. A further observation I should like to make is that the winning nation is also a social harmony. It's a nation capable of talking to its government and its workforce, and it's a nation which promotes an ongoing dialogue where people sit around a table and develop a structured approach to their future success. This, of course, must also be a global plan. It cannot focus solely within the EC. I would now like to move on and offer some comments on the need for excellence in industry and the private sector.

Our companies must strive for specialisation so that they can secure a place among the key specialised suppliers in a given field. Management must have a well developed vision. It's the vision from the top and the commitment from the top that are so important in setting the example. It's not just a question of saying it but also of believing and doing it. Market share is paramount for any company and we must therefore engage in continuous research and development in order to keep the technological edge. To do this we must have unique knowledge and skills. So, once again, it is a matter of education, education and education. And we must realise that education does not end when people have the papers in their hands from the high school, or the college or university. Rather, there is a moral obligation on both the employers and the government to make sure that they provide sufficient opportunities for people to grow in their knowledge and skills. For this to happen, we need a hands-on top management where the accent is on operational and product excellence. I have always been doubtful about those people who win millions of dollars in a paper operation in mergers and acquisitions. Indeed, I have my own personal doubts if such things are always on the ethical side. We must not lose sight of the importance of the production side, and the concept of value added. Top management must consider how they are going to take on this new large market of 320 million people, with all the tremendous opportunities this implies. Success will not be automatic. Let's not fool ourselves by thinking that the market is there and we just walk in. This new market is going to be hard work. We must develop our hidden strengths and evolve strategies to maintain domination in any given field. We must build on our strengths and diminish our weaknesses. Our strategy must be to access all Triad markets where we can find consumers who match the sophistication of our products. We cannot expect to make cheap things because in general such things are being made more easily elsewhere. We have a tradition in Western Europe of making good quality products and we must continue and develop this tradition through the formation of alliances when necessary. If there is some strength in Ireland and we lack this strength in Belgium, then we must find some mechanism whereby we could work in the same direction and co-operate together.

**Conclusion**

We live in an era of great change. There are for example a great number of disintegrating and disunifying pressures. Perhaps the best example is the situation in Eastern Europe where practically everything is disintegrating and disunifying. People seem to want to review existing concepts of nations, regions and so on. But there are also the integrating pressures. There is the EC and EFTA. There are the nations of the Arab World and there is ASEAN. Even the Americans are integrating, and as an illustration of this the US have recently signed a new trade agreement with the Canadians. Already, we have witnessed the emergence of a US/Canada trade bloc — and very soon Mexico will join them. Its going to be a powerful North American bloc — Mexico, United States and Canada as one market. The new president of Mexico has attempted to remove the complex that the Mexicans had vis-à-vis the US. He has told his people very clearly that 'we don't have a border there with enemies, we have a border with opportunites'. So the Mexicans have clearly chosen the side of North America. I would like to conclude then by suggesting that we are all faced with a tremendous challenge. Everything is changing; you only have to look at your television to see this. Everywhere there is the dynamic of change. The question now facing us is 'are we prepared to accept this dynamic of change?' Are we prepared to meet the challenges ahead? Very often if you want to look into the future, you must first look into the past. It is now more than 2,000 years since Socrates said 'he is not only idle who does nothing, but he is idle who might be better employed'. This is surely something to think about. There is a tremedous human potential, but human resources are very costly indeed, and I often wonder if we really employ people to the best of their abilities. In the public sector, for example, one wonders whether we are utilising the tremendous potential that is available and making full use of the people, the skills and the education. Furthermore what might happen if we could only achieve this synergy between the two sectors where people sit down and say 'let's take on this challenge, and let's find the right solutions'. For this, however, you need action. We need people who are really action-orientated and we need leadership. We need leadership on the government side, and on the industrial side. This is something that must be created and stimulated in order to ensure that the right people lead the way.

I would like to end on a positive note. We need more skilled and educated people because we have to address all of these issues and I think that in the context of the development of Europe, we will perhaps solve the problems better in a European way with our own distinctive European traditions. We live in a Europe which has entered a new phase of evolution. What will happen to Germany, for example, is not yet clear. However it seems unlikely that the shape and structure of the EC will remain uninfluenced by this new evolution. So we must keep our sense of perspective, and realise that there are tremendous problems ahead of us. Nevertheless we in business, and also you in government, are used to solving problems. Indeed this is the only way, the only clear path that I see to developing prosperity. There is no alterntive but to ensure that the driving forces of each country, that is the government, industry and people, must co-operate together in planning and shaping our common future.

MICHAEL WALSH

# Prosperity in Ireland — The Roles of Industry and Government

A coherent and well administered industrial policy will be a major factor affecting the ability of the Irish economy to create wealth and generate employment in the years ahead. It is only through the creation of wealth that we can improve the general economic welfare of our economy.

We have a long history of industrial policy in Ireland. Government intervention in the marketplace has been a major force behind the creation of an industrial base in Ireland and behind the fostering of industrial development.

However, industrial policy in Ireland is now about to enter an exciting new phase. This new phase will be brought about by the many changes which we can expect in the international business environment in the 1990s. The principal force of this change will be the completion of the internal market in 1992. Other forces of change will be the spread of information technology, the pace of technological change and general changes in demography and consumer preference. In the light of this the major challenge facing both Irish industry and Irish industrial policy over the 1990s will be to adapt and adjust to this new competitive environment.

My talk this afternoon will focus on what I see as the issues for Irish industrial policy into the 1990s. I will start with a brief review of the development and current state of Irish industrial policy and will try to put some perspective on our record in this area to date. I will also detail what I see as the major changes which we can expect to see in Irish industry over the next few years and will conclude with some views as to how we should adapt our current industrial policy to meet the challenges of the future. Adaptation in this context is a nice word for radical change.

**An introduction to industrial policy**

Industrial policy is currently, and has been for some time, the subject of a lively debate among Irish economists. Sharp divisions have emerged between those who favour active state intervention in stimulating and guiding industrial development and those who feel that such a policy is unlikely to raise economic welfare. The arguments for each side of this debate were first introduced in the late eighteenth and nineteenth centuries and have not changed significantly since. Needless to say the economists have changed the language, lest we might think they have done no work for the past 200 years.

There are two contrasting views of the problems facing Irish industrial development and of the appropriate government action to solve these problems. One side of the argument is that the economic environment in Ireland does not favour the development of industry, that existing government incentives are inadequate to compensate for this, and that government actions not primarily directed towards the industrial sector frequently have a harmful effect on industrial development. The other side of the argument is based on the belief that Ireland, in common with a number of other late-industrialising countries, faces significant barriers to entry into internationally competitive industries because of the advantages enjoyed by established competitors. These advantages relate mainly to economies of scale in production, marketing and finance, and to superior access to technology.

These two views, however are not mutally exclusive and in many instances, the differences between them are not as great as is often claimed. For example, it is generally accepted by both sides that it is inappropriate to focus our industrial policy on attempting to attract multinational subsidiaries. Rather, it is essential for us to focus on industrial policy towards strong internationally competitive indigenous industry. However, it is in the policy approaches to encouraging this indigenous industry that disagreement emerges.

Those who believe that our economic environment is not conducive to industrial development argue strongly that the government should concentrate on generating the correct environment for industrial activity. They should focus on developing an efficient and low-priced infrastructure, restraining increases in labour and other input costs and restructuring tax and grant incentives so as to encourage more investment and entrepreneurial effort in industry, rather than in other sectors which contribute less to national development.

On the other hand, people who believe that there are significant economies of scale in established industries, argue strongly that, because of the disadvantages faced by new Irish firms in breaking into many industries which are dominated by strong established foreign firms, few if any private enterprises in Ireland could attempt to do so on their own initiative, even when local conditions and government incentives are favourable. Consequently, fostering the correct industrial environment is in itself not sufficient. Government policy must assume a more active role. Rather than simply administering incentive schemes, development agencies must be prepared to take initiatives in developing new industries on a scale sufficient to overcome the barriers faced by a late-industrialising country. The success of industrial strategies in Japan, South Korea and Taiwan was based on this logic.

In an Irish context, while these two views may appear to be opposites, industrial policy, particularly in the 1990s, could be at its most effective if policy makers focus on the suitable elements of both within our overall industrial policy.

**Industrial policy - a look backwards**

Ireland has had a long history of industrial policy, or of government encouragement of and participation in industrial development. It started as early as the 1930s, when we relied on protectionism and a guaranteed domestic market to foster industrial growth and employment. This policy of protectionism achieved impressive results in the early years. However, the limits of this approach became apparent early in the post-war era.

The major impetus for a change in policy came in 1958 with the publication of the Government report 'Economic Development'. Set against the recession and emigration of the 1950s, this report concluded that 'policies hitherto followed, though given a fair trial, have not resulted in a a viable economy'. It heralded the switch to an outward looking policy based on export-led growth. The main elements of this policy still remain in place. They are: attraction of foreign investment, corporation profit tax concessions initially to exporting and later to all manufacturing firms, capital and other grants to new and expanding firms; absence of controls on foreign ownership of firms or on profit repatriation and free trade with Europe.

The experience of the 1960s and 1970s was, by most standards, highly successful. These were years of unprecedented and sustained economic and industrial growth. Between 1963 and 1973, manufacturing employment in Ireland rose at an average annual rate of 1.7%, almost three times the OECD average. During the 1970s Ireland had the highest rate of GDP growth in the European Community. Manufacturing industry was to the fore in this performance. Manufactured exports, for example, grew twice as rapidly as merchandise exports as a whole, while exports of manufactures (excluding food and drink) constituted 62 per cent of merchandise exports in 1981 as against 22 per cent in 1960. Government policy was not solely responsible for these achievements, of course. The favourable international economic environment up to the oil crises was an essential backdrop.

However, with the benefit of hindsight, we now know that this period was not one of unmitigated success. Subsequent problems in the major macroeconomic balances of external payments and governments finances are the central indicators of this. Clearly, these involve policies outside the domain of industry and industrial policy. Macroeconomic and industrial policies are, however, interrelated. Basically, Ireland's success over the 1970s, did not allow us to either avoid or overcome present economic difficulties. This is most clearly evident in looking at unemployment, the long standing central consideration in Irish economic policy. Over the 1970s, manufacturing industry despite the high growth in output, failed to deliver the goods in job terms. As the structure of industry in Ireland has changed, job gains in new firms have been outpaced by job losses in older firms.

All of this serves to highlight the one critical point which we should bear in mind for the future. Industrial policy and government intervention in industry cannot be divorced from the more general economic picture. An excellent industrial policy can only be effective in increasing the overall prosperity of our economy if it is implemented in the context of sensible and well thought out general economic policies. Our poor record over the late 1970s and early 1980s is due primarily to poor general economic planning in that period and not to any faults of our industrial policy. Therefore, now that we have succeeded in correcting our general economic policy, we must ensure that we keep this policy consistent into the 1990s, if our industrial policy, no matter how well thought-out, is to succeed.

**The changing structure of Irish industry**

One of the consequences of the outward-looking industrial policies of the 1960s and 1970s is that today the Irish economy is highly open to international trade, both exports and imports. This is particularly true in manufacturing industry. Over half of the output of manufacturing firms in Ireland is sold overseas, and this proportion is much higher in newer growth industries such as electronics and pharmaceuticals.

Together with this increase in openness, the past two decades have witnessed important structural changes in the Irish industrial sector. Older established, traditional industries have declined in importance. Industries such as textiles, clothing and footwear, and leather have been particularly affected with employment in these industries declining dramatically in the past decade. At the same time, employment in newly-established foreign-owned firms has shown a marked increase. These new foreign firms have increasingly tended to concentrate in the electronics and chemicals sectors and in most cases these new firms were subsidiaries of large multinational firms.

The emergence of Ireland as a base for export-orientated foreign firms, attracted by extensive financial incentives as well as free access to the EEC market, is reflected in this structural transformation of Irish manufacturing industry. However, although the employment contribution has been striking, there are a number of drawbacks which came with this policy of industrial development. The main drawbacks are that while producing a spohisticated product, a proportion of foreign owned firms use their Irish plant for only one stage in the manufacturing process: even when the entire product is manufactured in Ireland the key functions of marketing and of research and development are usually retained by the parent company; a large proportion of profits earned by foreign subsidiaries in Ireland may be repatriated by the parent firm, rather than invested in further expansion in this country; and foreign firms have tended to source most of their raw materials and intermediate inputs abroad. This leads to low linkages between foreign and domestic firms. Consequently, the potential spin-off contribution of multinational subsidiaries to the Irish economy is not maximised.

In addition to the above difficulties, which are common to most countries pursuing industrial policies based on the attraction of direct foreign investment, two major problems for policy in Ireland became increasingly obvious in recent years. The first was a decline in Ireland's relative attractiveness as a location for foreign industry. The failure of foreign industry to develop strong ties with the domestic economy meant that further employment increases depend on continuing high levels of new direct foreign investment. That decline in the relative attractiveness of Ireland at that time was a result of two major factors which occurred simultaneously in the early to mid 1980s. These factors were the existence of serious overcapacity in the international industrial environment and a dramatic increase in Irish labour costs due principally to rapid increase in both direct and indirect tax charges. In the period since then, however, these factors have now improved and many multinational companies will now confirm that Irish labour costs compare favourably internationally and consequently, we are regaining our share of direct international investment.

The second major problem for Irish industrial policy in that period was often argued to be the cost to the public finances of funding the industrialisation effort. As a result of the high rate of job loss which Ireland had experienced since 1973, the number of sustainable jobs created had fallen far short of the gross number of new jobs created. The result of this was that the cost per job sustained was significantly higher than average annual earnings per job. In foreign industry, it was approximately twice average earnings and in indigenous industry three times average earnings.

However, I would argue that the important issue here is not the short-term costs of the industrialisation programme but rather whether the cost over the longer term will prove to be worthwhile. The more immediate concern is the reason for the high rate of job loss. This issue was tackled by a number of studies which concluded that it could be attributed to a number of factors, not all of which were under domestic control.

One reason identified by the National Economic and Social Council (NESC) was that, particularly in the case of indigenous industry, insufficient attention was paid to the structure necessary for a company to remain viable. A more general explanation put forward by the OECD, was that the incentive schemes offered in Ireland had not been as efficiently directed as they might have been. This comment was particularly relevant in relation to the effects of incentives focused on reducing the cost of capital to firms. After allowing for inflation, it has been calculated that the cost of capital in 1983 was only about half of what it had been a decade earlier. Over the same period, labour costs increased quite rapidly, partly as a direct result of government decisions to increase payroll taxes, with the result that the substitution of capital for labour was encouraged. It is, therefore, not surprising that increases in industrial employment over that period were so modest and that the cost of sustainable jobs was so high.

**The current focus of industrial policy**

The difficulties and problems of the 1970s prompted a major re-examination of the aims and instruments of Irish industrial policy. The conclusion of this re-examination resulted in the Telesis Report, published in 1984, a report which is largely responsible for the current direction and focus of Irish industrial policy.

In general terms, The Telesis Report agreed with the broad thrust of Irish industrial policy up to that time, and was complimentary about many aspects of its implementation. However, Telesis raised many questions about how the government should influence industrial development and placed considerable emphasis on striking the correct balance between the promotion of foreign and indigenous industry.

The central point of the Telesis argument was that 'no country has successfully achieved high incomes without a strong base of indigenously owned resource or manufacturing companies in traded business'. In Telesis' view, Irish industrial policy devoted insufficient resources to developing indigenous businesses. It also argued that Ireland was paying too much in grants and tax forgone for the number and type of sustainable jobs which foreign firms brought.

The Telesis report formed the basis of the current focus of Irish industrial policy and was a major influence in the 1984 White Paper on Industrial Policy — the document which currently dictates government policy towards industry. In this White Paper, the key objectives of Irish industrial policy were laid down as follows:

1. To create and maintain the maximum number of sustainable jobs, as many as possible high-skilled, in manufacturing and international service industries.
2. To maximise value-added by these sectors and to capture the wealth thus created for further investment and employment creation in the Irish economy.
3. To develop a strong internationally competitive industrial sector in Ireland, made up of both Irish and foreign-owned industry.
4. To promote the more rapid development of our natural resource-based industries, particularly food and timber.
5. To promote the integration of foreign industry into the Irish economy through greater linkage with Irish industry and educational institutions.

These objectives reaffirmed the general thrust of industrial policy in Ireland over the period since 1960. The new policy was based on the premise that government intervention in the manufacturing sector is both necessary and desirable and that it should continue to take its already established form. It did not appear that any consideration was given to a radical change in approach, such as large scale public ownership of manufacturing industry or a dramatic reduction in the level of direct government support for industry, but merely represented a continuation of old ways.

However, two striking differences do exist with traditional industrial policy.

1. Employment creation is now only one of five objectives, relegated from its traditional position of dominance. This reflected the realisation that the potential for direct job creation in manufacturing was low and that the focus now was maximising domestic value added which would eventually lead to jobs elsewhere.
2. The emphasis is now on the international competitiveness of our industrial sector, again an emphasis which is a direct response to concern over the rapid rate of import penetration in Ireland in the 1980s and the high import

content of both domestic and foreign-owned export orientated industry.

The White Paper was an excellent response to the problems faced by Irish industry at that time. A number of the proposals implemented by the Paper were significant in that they represented a clear decision by policy-makers that government had a very important and central role to play in supporting smaller Irish firms to overcome the competitive barriers imposed by scale.

In this regard, the major developments were: the National Linkages Programme which was intended to encourage the development of sub-supply industries and which, among other things, provided for the co-ordination of State support and assistance for marketing, process development and quality control during the initial stages of a company's development; the Export Development Scheme which was designed specifically to address identified weaknesses and to help raise the levels of export performance of Irish firms and the initiation of the concept of 'picking winners' for the IDA.

The concept of 'picking winners' is perhaps the most significant of these, and if properly implemented, is a logical base from which to develop Irish industry into the 1990s. The scheme is motivated by the desire to build up and support strong Irish based companies which are capable of taking strategic decisions and achieving strong market positions in their respective international markets. In its most extreme form, it will involve the State acting in the role of venture capitalist, providing capital backing and managerial/marketing development assistance to firms who are chosen to be 'winners'.

Of course, the concept of picking winners is all very well in theory but will require careful implementation and a re-orientation of attitude amongst both the state sector and amongst the public if it is to be successful. For a start, the concept of picking winners is a slight misnomer. It is impossible to pick winners all the time. The best one can hope to do is select companies which have a better than average chance of success. There are still risks attached and it would be inappropriate not to recognise these risks. Nevertheless, the concept of picking winners can make a major impact on improving the thrust of industrial policy. Carefully selected backing of these winners can reduce the risks involved with this form of government involvement and will undoubtedly result in greater economic return on taxpayer's money. It will also give Irish industry an opportunity to compete effectively with foreign firms who do not suffer from the disadvantages of small scale.

**Industrial policy for the 1990s — a changing environment**

Industrial policy in Ireland is now entering a new phase in its development. What has served us well in the 1970s and 1980s may not necessarily be what is required for effective industrial policy in the 1990s. For one thing, the industrial environment will be substantially different in the 1990s and Irish firms will be facing very different challenges. The most important of these will be the creation of the internal market, which is scheduled to take place in 1992. The internal market, on completion, will give Irish firms access to a market of over 320 million people throughout Europe. Of course, it will also give European companies direct access to the Irish market and will significantly change the state of competition for many Irish firms. The internal market, however is only one change which is likely to affect Irish industry in the 1990s. Constant improvements in information technology, rapid rates of technological change, changing consumer preferences and demographic changes are all likely to have equally dramatic impacts.

The collective impact of these factors is likely to affect firms in different ways. These different effects can be broken into direct and indirect effects. The principal direct effects will be:

1. Cost reduction which will result from removal of non-tariff barriers on completion of the internal market. For example, firms should be able to find cheaper inputs, and items like transport, insurance and packaging and labelling costs should also fall. The cost reductions should facilitate price reduction and consequently increased demand and output.

2. Increased competition which will result from the improved market access of firms in all countries. As a consequence, firms which can currently operate high price-cost margins or price discrimination should find this ability curtailed. In short, firms will find it less easy to practice market segmentation.

The direct impact of these two factors will differ substantially from industry to industry and , indeed, will also affect different firms in different ways. For example, industries which are affected by high customs costs at present will benefit from sharp falls in cost in this area in the 1990s and consequently will be strongly affected by cost reductions. Similarly, firms which operate in concentrated industries at present will be more severely affected by increasing competition than those which operate in more open sectors.

Of perhaps greater importance to Irish industry, however, will be the likely secondary effects of these two forces. The principal secondary effects which come to mind in this area are:

1. Economies of scale: the increased demand and supply of goods, resulting from lower price may give rise to economies of scale for firms operating in certain industries. Typically, these economies of scale will result in larger low cost producers eliminating smaller high cost firms and thus initiating major industry restructuring or rationalisation. The size of economies of scale will determine what kinds of firms will reap the greatest medium to long term benefit from completion of the European market, and also what kinds of firms will emerge in Europe after completion of the internal market. If economies of scale, of whatever sort, are very substantial, then larger firms will have an initial advantage and very large firms will ultimately emerge. If economies of scale are not so significant then small to medium size enterprises will benefit, and completion will take some other form than that of scale-based cost reduction. Recognition of these impacts of economies of scale and of the industries which will be most affected by it will be a major determinant in developing successful industrial policy for the 1990s.

2. Removal of inefficiencies: where some degree of monopoly power exists then total costs of production may not be minimised. Sharper competition can bring about a removal of these inefficiencies. In addition, increased competition will act to reduce the element of monopoly profits being charged in those cases.

3. Increased innovation: firms faced with more aggressive competition will seek not only to match the competition by cost reductions but also to evade it by re-positioning themselves. Product differentiation usually requires innovation of some sort, and so the 1990s and the completion of the internal market will induce firms to innovate.

**How will this affect Irish firms?**

All of these changes will ,in various ways, have a dramatic impact on the playing field for Irish firms. However, they will affect each category of Irish firm in a different way. For the purpose of crude analysis I have broken up Irish industry as follows:

(1) foreign owned grant-aided export-orientated firms;
(2) large-scale, indigenous industry;
(3) fragmented indigenous industry;
(4) internationally traded industries.

These sectors, intended to represent a cross section of Irish industry, will be affected by the developments expected in the 1990s as follows:

1. foreign owned, grant aided, export orientated industry will benefit from cost reductions since many, while not protected, are hampered by customs barriers, technical standards, etc, and are also disadvantaged by high transport costs. They will also benefit from cost reduction as most are owned by major international players. However, the extent to which they will benefit from cost reductions will depend on where the Irish firms are in their parent's priorities.

2. large-scale, indigenous industry will benefit from cost reductions and in some cases, may benefit proportionately more so than their European counterparts. It will suffer from increased competition and will only be able to overcome this through developing products for overseas markets. Planning market strategy for these new products will be the key challenge and industrial policy can have a major role to play in this. Duplication will not necessarily succeed. Innovation will be essential.

3. fragmented indigenous industry. Import competition may pose a threat but many of these firms are in international industries with low barriers and as such may not be affected. Changes in process and product technology and consumer tastes may be more of a challenge. Most of these industries are closely linked to domestic demand and will benefit from other aspects of developments in the 1990s, principally expanding domestic demand.

4. internationally traded Industries. These industries are no longer protected and consequently may benefit somewhat from the removal of barriers protecting their competitors. The major challenge lies in developing competitive advantage for these firms through various combinations of product differentiation, production technology and information and marketing systems.

In summary, therefore, it should be clear from the above that the internal market and changes in the international business environment of the 1990s will affect all aspects of Irish industry. It will affect various firms in different ways depending on their particular industry and their position within it, and while completion of the internal market in 1992 will be a major force, it would be foolish to focus entirely on 1992. This is only one change feature of the business environment. For many businesses other factors such as technical change, innovation and demographic changes will be far more important than 1992 and our industrial policy should also address these developments as they arise.

**What does this imply for industrial policy in the 1990s?**

As I have already said, I believe that the thrust of Ireland's industrial policy over the recent past, and in particular in the period since the 1984 White paper, has been correctly focussed. I believe that we have been correct to focus on building up strong indigenous enterprises rather than depend on the 'easy option' mobile foreign investment and I believe that the correct approach to developing these indigenous industries has been to encourage them in the home market and identify barriers to entry which they may face in overseas markets. The challenge for industrial policy is to design policy interventions which assist our indigenous firms in overcoming these barriers. We have been relatively successful in doing this to date and Irish industrial policy in the 1990s will be most effective if we continue to be pro-active in our search for ways around the entry barriers.

However, there are a number of areas which, as a result of the changing environment of the 1990s perhaps need more attention in industrial policy in future years. These are set out below.

**(1) The competitive importance of scale**

One of the most obvious, and possibly most far-reaching changes in the business environment of the 1990s will be the process of rationalisation and consolidation which will take place as a result of the completion of the internal market.

Rationalisation and economies of scale are trends which have been evident in European industry over the past number of years. However, in Ireland, over past decades, instead of larger Irish producers eliminating or absorbing smaller producers as they orientated themselves to a growing market, the size structure of Irish industry has become less concentrated. Consequently, scale must become a more important concern of industrial policy than it has up to now. In particular, industrial policy should focus on assisting firms in reaching the required scale in industries where the absence of scale means that survival is not possible; providing support in overcoming the size disadvantage where it relates to a single dimension of the business, for example, production scale, and assisting firms in identifying market segments where they can escape the scale factor — e.g. a niche strategy where product differentiation can be pursued.

A key feature of developing a strategy to overcome the problems of economies of scale is the realisation that economies of scale will affect different industries in different ways. Consequently, policy measures for different industries should also vary.

The paragraphs below give some broad guidelines on how various sectors of the Irish economy are likely to be affected by scale factors.;

*Manufacturing industry:* economies of scale exist in most large scale production orientated manufacturing industries.

Foreign competitors, many of them semi-state operations, will have advantages in this area. Irish firms will find it increasingly difficult to compete. However, sub-supply industries can survive independently and niche operators will also survive. The key is identifying the niches.

*Food/agribusiness:* Economies of Scale do exist in production/distribution. However, access to raw materials and strong brands mean that niche operators will remain viable.

*Financial services:* Research is divided on whether economies exist here. If they do they are more likely to exist in wholesale financial services. Retail financial services will still be highly dependent on local presence.

*Service operations:* Generally relate to people businesses where economies are more difficult to crystalise.

**(2) A focus on innovation**

Another important aspect of competition in the 1990s will be the drive towards innovative activity. Many industries are already undergoing a major wave of technical change which is likely to continue for some time. Research in other countries has shown that firms in peripheral regions undertake significantly less innovation, especially product innovation, than firms in more central regions.

There is therefore a strong case to be made for developing industrial policy in Ireland in line with support for innovation. Key aspects of the support might be the development of the telecommunications infrastructure as a basis for the widespread adoption of information technology; the role of management in identifying opportunities for innovation and in implementing changes in firm's activities, and stimulation of the innovation process itself.

**(3) Management development**

No industrial policy will succeed, no matter how well thought out, unless Irish management have the ability to effectively guide their firms through the competitive battlefield. At present, in many areas, the level of management development in Ireland is unacceptably low, given the economic challenges that face the country. This is a situation which must change and, while it can be adressed in other aspects of government policy, there should also be a place for it within industrial policy for the 1990s. A co-operative approach to management education and development should be a priority, and this could easily be put in place in conjunction with other bodies, such as the universities, the IMI and the IPA.

**(4) Marketing**

Another important focus on industrial policies for the 1990s should be the development of an effective marketing strategy for Ireland. Effective marketing of our strengths as a base for industry has been very successful for Ireland in the past and it has proven to be a very cost-efficient way of attracting foreign industry to Ireland. In the long run, the best advertisement for Ireland as a base for industrial activity will be the success of Irish firms in international markets. However, for the present, international marketing campaigns can continue to be important features of our industrial policy.

The marketing drive for the International Financial Services Centre has perhaps been the best recent example of the effectiveness of well-planned marketing and for a limited outlay of public money has established Ireland as a high quality base for international financial services. The influx of foreign firms to the centre is testament to its success to date.

**Other aspects**

However, these elements of a new industrial policy for the 1990s will only be really effective if they are accompanied with a significant re-examination of the roles which state agencies and the government itself have to play in future industrialisation.

A fundamental element of industrial policy for the 1990s must be the introduction of a pro-active drive within all government agencies to provide positive business attitudes in the country. The financial services industry is a key example of this. Within this industry everyone, including the Revenue Commissioners, has a development attitude. It is not often that one thinks of the Revenue Commissioners as a development agency but it is important to realise that much of business has a tax dimension and it is only by looking at the number of companies who conduct their business through Holland or Belgium that one realises the importance of a business development orientation. A similar attitude among Irish agencies would be a valuable component of our overall industrial strategy.

Our state agencies also have a major role to play in future industrialisation.In this regard, the Taoiseach's initiative, whereby our state agencies are now being encouraged to invest in other areas of activity, is a major development. Many of our semi-states are presently operating in areas which do not offer exciting growth opportunities. These semi-states are often in a better position, because of their commercial experience and their ownership role, to identify new development opportunities. Toptech, a recent joint venture between the ESB and Aer Lingus is an excellent first step in this direction. Toptech has been established to exploit a perceived opportunity in the supply of services to manufacturers of metallic components for the computer peripherals industry. The company has the strong capital and management backing of the ESB and Aer Lingus and has already licenced the relevant technology and commenced operations. With the support of such parties, it must certainly have very promising prospects.

In the context of these developments, it also makes sense for us to re-examine the roles of our existing government agencies in assisting industrial development. In the context of the 1990s, and if one expects economies of scale to become a major competitive factor, then perhaps it makes little sense to pursue a fragmented approach to grant aiding a wide range of industry.

In summary, I believe that an appropriate industrial policy has a major role to play in the prosperity of Ireland in the 1990s. I believe that such an industrial policy should focus on creating an appropriate domestic base for industry in Ireland. It should do this through developing an efficient and low priced infrastructure, restraining increases in labour and other input costs and restructuring incentives to encourage productive investment.

However, to be effective, industrial policy must also be flexible to adapt to the changing business environment of the 1990s. This will involve developing strategies to recognise the increasing importance of scale, the need for constant innovation, the necessity of effective management and the benefits of international marketing.

Of course, a good industrial policy can only be effective in the context of sound general economic policies, and this is as important a challenge for us in the 1990s as any other aspect of our strategy for this decade.

AIDAN O'BOYLE

# Ireland within Europe in the 1990s — An Assessment

THE development of an internal market in Europe by 1992 is currently the subect of great debate. The NESC report on 'Ireland in the European Community' analyses our performance to date; the likely impact on business and industry and the strategies which might be utilised to position ourselves successfully in this single market. Least enthusiastic of all perhaps are the Finance Ministers of the EC-12 who recognise the Exchequer implications associated with the proposals for Value Added Tax harmonisation and approximation of excise duties. Dilution of the Commission's original fiscal proposals is now well under way and one questions how the physical barriers within this EC market of twelve can be eliminated in the absence of indirect tax approximation.

However it is not my intention to dwell on the 1992 theme. I would like instead to take stock of where we are today and the key considerations which will enable Irealand to fulfil its true potential in the enlarging community of the 1990s.

Participation in the European Community since 1973 has affected the manufacturing, service and agricultural sectors in different ways. However, the following broad statements can be made.

1. Trade has diversified over the past sixteen years with a growing emphasis on exports to continental EC countries. The opportunities for further diversificaton are soundly based on the strong purchasing power which continental EC countries display. (See Table 1).

2. Membership of the European Moneary System has resulted in the Irish pound being successfully linked to the German Deutschmark. We have accepted the disciplines associated with such a linkage and have seen

major progress in the programme to reduce public sector borrowing. The CII is targeting a borrowing requirement of 1.5% of GNP for 1990.

3. Unemployment has now peaked and the growth in employment is steadily accelerating. We would expect a growth in net employment of some 15,000 in 1989. Such growth should be sustained throughout the 1990s if we can successfully exploit our membership of a growing European Community.

4. Inflation, which dipped to an all-time low of 2.1% in 1988, has doubled over the past twelve months. Care must be taken to ensure that this trend does not continue and that domestic consumption is brought into line with economic output.

Table 1: **Geographical distribution of Irish exports**
(Percentage Shares)

| | 1972 | 1988 |
|---|---|---|
| UK | 61 | 35 |
| Other EC | 17 | 39 |
| Total EC | 78 | 74 |
| Other | 22 | 26 |

The prognosis for our successful participation in the developing European market has been significantly improved over the past two years and this is due in no small measure to the agreement between the Social Partners as contained in the Plan for National Recovery. However, the European experiment is in many senses just beginning. I could envisage that during the course of the 1990s the European Community will expand to include Austria, Turkey, Norway, Sweden and Finland. Who is to say whether it will not in time embrace some of the reforming economies of Eastern Europe? Thus the EC map of the year 2000 may well encompass a population in excess of 428 million.

Our successful participation in that broader framework rests ultimately on three key elements: (1) People; (2) Land; (3) Environment.

**The people factor**

The dynamic underlying successful industrial development in the Europe and Ireland of tomorrow depends on the successful application of the new information technologies, not just as they apply to the hightech sectors of microelectronics, telecommunications, advanced materials and biotechnology, but in the application of these generic technologies to upgrading the competitiveness of our traditional sectors. These sectors include clothing, footwear, wood products and the natural resource based industries, including food, aquaculture, marine, and forestry. Underpinning the application of such technologies is the availability of trained brain power; our graduates and diploma holders in science and engineering. The recent decision by Intel and Motorola to establish major production facilities in Ireland is based very much on the people factor.

The latest First Destination Awards show a growing demand for science and technology graduates/diploma holders. At the same time incipient skill shortages in the science and technology area are now appearing, as evidenced in a recent CII survey which showed that 55% of companies surveyed encountered varying degrees of difficulty in finding suitable people to fill vacant positions.

The Confederation recommends that funding should now be provided to increase Irish participation in third level education to 50% of the relevant age cohort by 1993 compared with about 25% today, and that this increase should be focused on the qualifications in greatest demand, for example engineering, computer science and business studies. Such investment in education should be seen in the framework of the overall allocation of state resources as between education, training and unemployment. (See Table 2).

Opposition to such additional investment in third-level education has tended to stem from the high level of graduate migration. Thus the latest First Destination Awards show that 19.9% of all third level award holders and up to 40% of science and engineering graduates have obtained employment abroad in 1988. Conservative reaction tends to say that additional investment in education may be lost to the Irish economy through such migration and that we should therefore not allocate additional resources to this area. What a narrow stance! Such a view fails to recognise that our sucessful participation in the Europe of the 1990s will be significantly enhanced by the creation of a network of Irish in Europe, which I believe will one day rival the network built up over many decades in the United States. Who is to say that the managing director of Thomson CSF or Siemens or Philips in 2005 will not be Irish?

Table 2: **Industry recruitment by academic disciplines Third level award holders**

| Discipline | 1988 Number | 1988 % Share | 1988/87 % Change |
|---|---|---|---|
| Engineering | 638 | 42.2 | +34.6 |
| Business Studies | 333 | 22.0 | +11.4 |
| Science | 356 | 23.5 | +38.0 |
| Art & Social Science | 93 | 6.2 | +16.2 |
| All Other Disciplines | 93 | 6.2 | +6.6 |
| Total Industrial Recruitment | 1513 | 100.0 | +29.5 |

The concept that we can participate meaningfully in the Europe of tomorrow without knowing it by experience is both naive and foolish. Such a developing network offers the dual advantage of growing market knowledge and experience on the ground in Europe as well as a developing reservoir of talent and experience for investment at home in the future. Now is not the time , therefore to cut back on educational investment but in fact to increase such investment in human capital, which will ultimately be refunded many times over in the years to come.

Let us for once think strategically and view our migrant youth as key contributors to an Irish network in Europe which can in the shorter term provide essential marketing and technological links for Irish business and industry and ultimately in the years ahead, be the cornerstone for enterprise creation at home. When we here in Ireland have created an environment conducive to enterprise and innovation, then many of these young people will return enriched by their experience both culturally, linguistically and technologically. The narrow thinking of the 1950s must now be banished from the Irish psyche. The youth of today are educated and enterprising. Let us treat them as such. But let us not forget that the competition in Europe for our talented young people is growing. While the population of the EC 12 will increase from 320 million in 1989 to 330 million in 2000, this hides the fact that the population of the Federal Republic of Germany will decline by 1.2 million in that period, with a growing proportion of aged. If we want to keep our young people at home then we must urgently address the disincentive effect of the high marginal personal tax rates in Ireland within the framework of an overall reform of the tax system.

Every effort must now be made to identify the participants in such an Irish network in Europe. In this regard I very much welcome the exciting initiative by the High Skills Pool, a project under the aegis of the Bolton Trust, to set up a comprehensive database of some 7,000 Irish graduates working abroad, detailing their present employment and relevant experience. The Finns have been in the forefront of countries appreciating the importance of such national networks overseas and it is high time we caught up.

Unfortunately, such strategic thinking is little in evidence today as shown by the number of schemes for graduate placement and training which have, I believe, been arbitrarily abolished since the beginning of 1989. Thus state support for the European Orientation Programme operated by the CII, which placed young Irish graduates in industry in Europe to gain both business and linguistic experience, was abolished at the beginning of 1989. I am concerned that the importance of languages for successful participation in the growing Europe of the 1990s is still not sufficiently appreciated. We are fifteen years in the European community and yet a recent Eurobarometer survey showed that 80% of Irish people are still unable to follow a conversation in any foreign language. Priority must now be given to ensuring that second level schools in Ireland be provided with the resources to ensure that all pupils have the opportunity to learn two modern continental languages and that all primary schools are required to teach one modern continental language.

The Science and Technology Employment Programme (STEP) which placed science and technology graduates/diploma holders in small and medium sized indigenous enterprises, has likewise been abolished. The ability of indigenous enterprises, particularly SME's to participate in EC cooperative programmes for R & D and technology transfer depends ultimately on having the science and technology graduates capable of integrating and adopting such technology to their company needs. A major impetus should now be given to supporting the Techstart Programme run by Eolas to ensure the annual placement of 200 graduate/diploma holders in science and technology in indigenous SME's.

The time has now come to recognise the key role which people and education will play in our economic development within the Europe of the 1990s. It is not a reduction in educational investment which is now required but an increase.

**The land factor**

Development of a comprehensive land use policy in Ireland, has, I must confess, been an aspiration as yet to be fulfilled. In the 1970s when Community funds could provide a ready market through intervention and price guarantees, the need for a market-led approach to land mobilisation appeared unnecessary. In the Europe of tomorrow, situated as it is within an international community seeking major changes in the support mechanisms for agriculture, a new impetus to alternative land use must now be given. We need to maximise the return we can obtain from this key resource. Emphasis over the past 15 years has been on volume production of commodity products, rather than added value consumer products for Continental markets. This emphasis is now changing in the light of changes in the CAP but must be seen against the reality that European food demand over the next twenty years will be static or will even fall due to only small increases in total populations, increases in the proportion of elderly (with lower food needs), and a decreased muscular activity due to labour saving technology (less walking less housework, and less industrial work). In terms of expenditure a small increase of around 0.5% per annum is projected up to the year 2000. This is not to say of course, that certain convenience food niche markets will not grow at a higher rate. Of course they will. However for Irish enterprises to take a market share in such a situation will, I believe, require acquisition of retail and distribution networks in continental markets. To fund such acquisitions will require further rationalisation in the agribusiness sector of Irish Industry. Nowhere is this more relevant and urgent than in the dairy sector.

The advent of the biosociety which heralds so many opportunities in the years to come in transforming under-utilised land and raw materials to produce new products in the chemicals, energy, pharmaceuticals, food and medical area, demands an urgent reassessment of land use policy. That a million hectares of agricultural land is still available for forestry development, sixty years after the foundation of the state is, I believe, of serious concern. The Europe of the 1990s will have a major deficit in wood products, second only to its imports of oil. Ireland can help to meet those needs. It will, however require a clear and enlightened national policy on overall land use. It is not for the European Community to define such a policy. In many ways the European community is as ambivalent about forestry as we have been at national level over many years.

We need a comprehensive land use policy which looks not only at the economic aspects of land use, but at the social implications of such use. Why would a farmer benefitting from the dole and a medical card risk their loss through economic exploitation of underutilised land. He has no reason to do so and to date has not done so. Thus exploitation of the undoubted potential which Ireland offers for wood and energy supply in the Community of the 1990s rests ultimately on the development of a national land use policy taking clear cognisance of the social aspects of such a policy.

**The environment factor**

Bypassed by the industrial revolution, Ireland has today an environment second to none in Europe which represents an unsurpassable asset for economic development in the 1990s.

To capitalise on such opportunites we will, however have to address the current concerns of the public at large on environmental issues. Such concerns can ultimately only be successfully addressed within the framework of a national policy on environmental protection and development. That such an overall policy has never seen the light of day is an indictment of governments of every hue in recent years.

These concerns, which to date have tended to focus on the chemical/pharmaceutical sectors of Irish industry, must be the remit of industry as a whole. However, we must be both balanced and realistic. Waste is a reality of industrial production.While clean technology can reduce the amount of waste produced it cannot eliminate it. It is the responsibility of the community as a whole to assume responsibility for the economically sound and environmentally safe disposal of such industrial waste. Reaction in recent years in Ireland would tend to suggest that this is the sole responsibility of industry, since any attempt to establish engineered sites for the disposal of industrial waste is met by vocal and persistent local opposition. If we want the benefits of modern products, be they pharmaceuticals, films, or the non-stick frying pan, then the community as a whole must accept responsiblity for their safe and environmentally acceptable disposal. The CII in January 1988 clearly defined the environmental principles which should underpin industrial development in the 1990s. These principles are:

1. Economic Development: Environmental policy should form an integral part of any strategy for overall economic and industrial development.

2. Prevention is Better than Cure: Industry must accept its responsibilities in regard to all aspects of the physical environment, including its visual, aesthetic, cultural and archaeological characteristics.

3. Economic costs versus real environmental risks: Legislation aimed at maintaining a clean environment must always balance the economic cost of pollution control measures against the real risk of damage to health and the environment.

4. Environmental Legislation - Uniform Implementation: Where environmental legislation is introduced, it should be consistently and uniformly enforced.

5. Maintenance of Constructive Dialogue with an Taisce and other Representative Environmental Organisations: Industry must involve an Taisce, other representative environmental organisations and the general public in the environmental planning process. Pre-planning consultations with local authorities, IDA, Eolas, An Taisce and the local community should be encouraged.

The public perception now exists that the environmental planning process is no longer working effectively. Such a perception is damaging the image of Irish industry and must be addressed as a matter of urgency. It will require the establishment of an independent environmental agency which will assess the results of monitoring carried out by industry in compliance with the licensing and planning requirements; carry out spot checks on industry's environmental monitoring equipment and procedures; assist local authorities in their task of implementing environmental impact assessment procedures; advise local authorities on the suitability of industrial locations for environmentally sensitive projects; develop periodic reports on the overall environmental situation in their regions, and set and enforce environmental standards.

While such an independent environment agency, with the key criteria of being both competent and independent, will help to restore confidence in the planning process, it is not of itself the full solution.

Our ability to capitalise on the tourist potential offered by the expanding Community market of the 1990s will depend ultimately on the general public's real commitment to overall environmental protection and development. This will involve a major educational process to educate the community at large to the need for eliminating litter, tidying up our towns and villages, preventing bungalow blight, and finally recognising that the environment is everybody's business.

Our successful development in the Europe of the 1990s will depend on our ability to exploit both our manufacturing and service industry (including tourism) capabilities. In my belief there is no reason why this cannot be achieved with a balanced approach based on sound Government policy and direction. Such direction must include a clear environmental policy statement from Government rather than a piecemeal approach to specific issues.

In the Europe of the 1990s, if we can capitalise on these three key inputs, namely people, land and the environment, then Ireland's future in a developing Europe is extremely positive.